Birds of North America

Savannah Sparrow's Nest   (Great Spruce Head Island, Maine)

Eliot Porter

Birds of North America
A Personal Selection

E. P. Dutton & Co., Inc. / New York / 1972

Also by Eliot Porter

In Wildness Is the Preservation of the World
The Place No One Knew: Glen Canyon on the Colorado
Forever Wild: The Adirondacks
Summer Island
Baja California: The Geography of Hope
Galapagos: The Flow of Wildness
Down the Colorado
Appalachian Wilderness
The Tree Where Man Was Born | The African Experience

Published, 1972, in the United States by E. P. Dutton & Co., Inc., New York,
and simultaneously in Canada by Clarke, Irwin & Co., Ltd., Toronto and Vancouver.

First Edition   Second Printing

Library of Congress Catalog Card Number: 72-82698

Printed in association with Chanticleer Press, Inc., New York,
and Amilcare Pizzi, S.P.A., Milan, Italy.
SBN: 0-525-06698-5

Acknowledgments

To Dr. and Mrs. W. Powell Cottrille, Dr. Lawrence H. Walkinshaw, William Dyer, and Edward M. Brigham, Jr., for their assistance in the field in bird finding; to all members of my family for their patience and understanding over a period of many years; to Crawford H. Greenewalt for generously making available the circuitry for the photoelectric control of camera equipment which facilitated flight photographs; and to R. P. Schwenker for manufacturing the electronic devices, I owe especial gratitude.

Black and white photographs appear on pages 49-56 and 89-96.

COMMON EGRET *Casmerodius albus* (Everglades, Florida: 1954)

SPARROW HAWK ♀ *Falco sparverius* (Santa Fe, New Mexico: 1958)

PURPLE GALLINULE *Porphyrula martinica* (Everglades, Florida: 1954)

GREAT-HORNED OWL *Bubo virginianus* (Tesuque, New Mexico: 1951)

WHISKERED OWL *Otus trichopsis* (Chiricahua Mountains, Arizona: 1959)

BURROWING OWL *Speotyto cunicularia* (Kissimmee Prairie, Florida: 1954)

EASTERN BLUEBIRD ♂ *Sialia sialis* (Winnetka, Illinois: 1942)   15

WINTER WREN *Troglodytes troglodytes* (Great Spruce Head Island, Maine: 1969)

Introduction

Birds have always attracted man by their brilliant colors, songs and other vocalizations, and especially by their unique possession of feathers adapted to flight. The attribute of flight has had more influence on human thought and aspiration than any other animal characteristic. From Daedalus and Icarus to Leonardo da Vinci, the ability to fly has excited man's envy. Though we have sought to attain the freedom of birds through technology as well as myth and fantasy, we have never succeeded in overcoming our earthbound limitation. A traveler strapped in his cramped seat will readily concede that the airplane is a far cry from the unrestrained flight of a bird.

For me, a love of birds developed steadily along lines not usually regarded as justifying a full-time profession. I have always been a great deal more affected by the beauty of birds than by the mysteries and unanswered questions concerning their classification and behavior. From time to time I have found myself concerned with bird behavior, but not with the single-minded dedication of the scientist. I soon discovered that the most satisfactory outlet for expressing my excitement over birds was the camera, rather than either pencil or brush. The camera is an instrument for immediate results, and by focusing my attention on the subject it offers a way of sublimating the indefinable longing that is aroused in me by close association with birds.

Bird photography is a pursuit that involves one in long hours of quiet sitting in the woods or in a blind which inevitably affords an opportunity for observing not only the behavior of the birds being photographed but of the activities of other birds and animals. The secret of wildlife observation is obvious enough—and, in truth, no secret at all—for it merely requires close attentiveness to all the minutiae of what goes on around one, made possible by a stillness of posture so that to other creatures one becomes just another object in nature. On numerous occasions I have found myself treated like an inanimate feature of the environment until I moved, when my fortuitous companion with whom I had begun to feel I had established a rapport suddenly took fright. This happened in a most striking manner years ago in May in New Hampshire. Although the month was well advanced, spring had not yet fully developed as is so often the case with the unpredictable New England spring. The fields were still more brown than green as the new blades of grass were just beginning to show through the sere winter cover. Shad trees were in full bloom, looming ghosts through the iron-gray tree trunks of lowland wood lots, but alder buds had not burst, delayed by the cold trapped in the swampy hollows. Only the wooded hillsides offered the new green of spring, a thin liquid veil cast over the forest.

I had walked down the slope of one of these fields of withered grass to the edge of an alder bog where the land broke off sharply dropping into watery thickets. It was a good place from which to look down into the bushes for migrating warblers that had been arriving in increasing numbers every night for a week. While I was engaged searching for new species I had not seen that year, I heard a rustling, slushing sound out in the bog apparently made by some medium-sized animal working its way through the underbrush. I thought it might be a dog. As I peered intently toward the noise I saw a brown furry body push through the alder stems in my direction. It came on straight to where I stood on the bank, and I saw that it was a large woodchuck followed by four young woodchucks in single file. Without hesitation—much to my surprise—she ascended the bank coming out on top, almost at my feet. Every moment I expected her to see me and charge away in panic, but as I stood there stone still, hardly breathing, she walked right past me within inches of my feet and headed out into the field. To her I was just an inert object. The first two young ones were following close behind her and all three had already gone several yards beyond me before the third little woodchuck had reached the top of the bank. When he got to my feet he stood up on his haunches to see better what direction his mother had taken. Because he was young and not very steady on his hind legs he placed a paw against my trousers for better balance. On seeing his mother and his two siblings he dropped down again on all fours and hurried after them. When the fourth baby came along I detained him by placing my field glasses—not my hand for I respected his young teeth—in front of his nose. He hissed and squealed flashing those teeth at me so aggressively that I was thankful for my instinctive caution. His mother hearing his cries of distress looked back over her shoulder to see what trouble he was in, and, seeing me for the first time, hurried on without more delay towards the safety of her den in the field, abandoning her improvident child to his fate. He galloped after her as soon as I let him go. I have had many such experiences in the field to remind me how easy it is for man to observe wildlife by becoming one with the natural landscape.

My first groping efforts as a photographer were exclusively of birds. After many years my interest in photography became more general, only to return to birds as my skill improved and as advances were made in photographic technology. It was not long before I realized that the criteria of excellence applied by ornithologists in this field were considerably below the high professional standards required of photographers in other fields. To raise the standards of bird photography called for the adoption of innovations and techniques developed for other purposes, notably the use of flash lamps synchronized with a high-speed shutter. This technological improvement, however necessary, was far from sufficient in itself. What was needed was essentially to raise bird photography above the level of reportage, to transform it into an art. With these concepts in mind, I went to work as a bird photographer. After gradually accumulating a sizable collection of prints, it was naturally my ambition to see them published. At the time I lived in Cambridge, where I taught at Harvard Medical School. In 1941 I took a portfolio to a Boston publisher, where an editor for whom birds were an avocation looked at them all, made encouraging comments, and then pronounced his edict on my work. "We cannot publish these," he said "because they are in black and white, and the birds cannot be unequivocally identified." I must have shown my disappointment, for he went on to suggest that he could publish my photographs if they were in color. I am sure he had no conception of the problems entailed in making color photographs of birds in 1941. Nevertheless, I took his remark as a sort of promise, and went to Eastman Kodak Company for advice on using synchronized flash along with Kodachrome film, which had recently appeared on the market.

That spring, I began photographing birds in color. A Guggenheim Fellowship for the project followed, and after I had learned to make color prints using the wash-off relief process, the precursor of dye-transfer prints, I returned to Boston with a portfolio of color prints in which I took inordinate pride. I was admitted to the same editor's office, and again he looked at the collection, making comments that were still more enthusiastic than before. But he said nothing about publishing them, until in an agony of suspense I asked a direct question. In reply he said, "We can't publish these, it would cost far too much."

In this book, published together for the first time, is my personal selection of the bird portraits I have struggled with and worried over for nearly half a century.

Eliot Porter
April, 1972

One

The best time to photograph birds is while they are rearing their young, when their behavior is most predictable and their foraging areas are restricted by territorial necessity. Also, because of a molt preceding the breeding season, many birds are in their most brilliant plumage at that time. Obviously, before any photography except of the most chancy sort can begin, the birds' nests, which for several weeks will be the center of their activities, must be found. This part of the photographer's work is by far the most time-consuming and, perhaps paradoxically, the most enjoyable, for it keeps him out in the open in wild places for hours at a time. Others things being equal—including knowledge of the birds and their habits—the number of nests found is directly proportional to the time spent searching. The first necessity, especially in finding the nests of particular species, is ability to identify the birds visually. Nearly as important is skill in recognizing specific songs. Singing during the breeding period has a special significance in that it marks the territory of the breeding pair and tells the observer that the bird in question has at least tentatively established itself in the region and will probably nest there.

In most species, song is an exclusive attribute of the male. He arrives first on migration and selects a locality where he will court a later-arriving female, mate with her, and determine where the nest is to be built. He roughly delineates the area by singing at various points around its circumference, indicating what he is prepared to defend against intrusion by other individuals of his species. Territorial information is invaluable knowledge for the photographer. But in addition, he must also become familiar with the habits of birds on their nesting grounds, their habitat adaptations, their manner of nesting, the kinds of sites they prefer, and the structure of their nests—the materials used and how they are put together. Before all this knowledge can be applied to the actual discovery of a nest, the photographer must be familiar with the geographical distribution of birds, their climatic preferences, their broad ecological needs and adaptations. It would be folly to search for forest-adapted species in the arid Southwest, or conversely for desert types in New England. Even within one of these regions, time would be wasted looking for arboreal birds in meadows.

Locating the nest of a small passerine bird does not guarantee that one will obtain photographs. Many hurdles still remain to be cleared. When the nest is still being constructed or the eggs are still being incubated, it is probable that the female will desert if she is unduly disturbed; or, as a result of the disturbance, the eggs may be destroyed by predators. Among birds, these predators are most often jays and grackles, whereas squirrels and chipmunks are the chief destroyers of birds' eggs among mammals. Depredations by mice, shrews, weasels and snakes are also common causes of nesting failure. In view of all these hazards, it should be obvious that the bird photographer cannot count on obtaining photographs before he has actually taken them. Nor can he afford to be complacent over having found a single nest. In my own experience, the toll of predation on warblers' nests found has often been as high as 75 percent, and under certain unfavorable conditions it may rise to 100 percent. Such losses are discouraging, to say the least, and should warn the novice against unguarded optimism.

The time to photograph birds at their nests promising the greatest likelihood of success is after the eggs have hatched. Then the adults are actively feeding the young and are least likely to desert the nest despite the presence and activities of the photographer. This is also the period in which the search for nests is most likely to be rewarded, as the parent birds' frequent journeys to the nest with food inadvertently reveal its location to an intent observer. From the photographic standpoint, finding a nest with young is likewise the most favorable circumstance since photography may be initiated without delay. When I find a nest in the early stages of the nesting period, I always wait until the young are three or four days old before setting up my equipment—although this is an anxious time, when all hope of securing photographs could be dashed by predation or an unforeseeable accident.

At this point the photographer bears a great responsibility to avoid jeopardizing the successful rearing of the young birds. If while operating his equipment he observes that things at the nest are not going well for the family, that the young are not being fed frequently enough, or are exposed too long to sun, rain or cold, he should withdraw at once. He may be able to return later, but he should do so with the utmost caution.

Once again, the steps necessary to safeguard the welfare and even the lives of the subjects may take up more time than the photography itself. This was my experience in June, 1971, at Kanawha State Park near Charleston, West Virginia, where I set out early one morning to photograph hooded warblers at their nest in a greenbrier vine. Since the young birds were only three days old, it would have been better to wait for two or three days, but I could not since I was leaving the next day. To allow time for unforeseen developments, I started to set up my camera and flash equipment at about 8:30. While I was thus occupied, the female scolded nearby. Before I loaded the camera or turned on the flash lamps, I sat down at what seemed a reasonable distance to watch her reaction. She flew around behind the nest in great agitation, flicking her wings and tail and chipping constantly, but never coming within ten feet of the greenbrier vine except once, when she landed on it above the nest—only to fly away again at once. A male hooded warbler sang in the distance, but none appeared near the nest. The female's behavior indicated that my presence alarmed her more than the camera did; to eliminate myself as a factor in her alarm I set up a blind, but still she would not go to the nest. Even after I had removed the camera and lights, leaving only the tripod, she appeared as fearful as ever.

The time was now 10:30. I was beginning to be concerned for the welfare of the young birds; the day was cool, and they had been unattended for more than two hours. I then removed all equipment from near the nest, carrying it a hundred feet back into the woods. But completely removing all strange objects from the vicinity of the nest (the blind was seventy-five feet away) had little effect on the behavior of the female; she continued to flutter nervously around the greenbrier vine, approaching a bit closer but still not daring to go to the nest. It was now noon, and when at last the male came with food and tried to feed the young birds, they were too cold and lethargic to open their mouths. After poking at them repeatedly without any response, he flew away. Meanwhile the female fluttered up to the vine without alighting, and then flew off with her mate.

At this point my conscience told me that I should give up any further attempt at photography. Being now responsible for the plight of the young warblers, however, I was obliged to do everything I could to make sure they survived. Since they could die of cold and exposure if the female did not soon return to brood her young, I took the part of a surrogate mother. Removing the four naked, cold, nearly lifeless nestlings, I held them cupped in my hand for ten minutes while I warmed them with my breath. When they had once more become lively, I replaced them in the nest and resumed my vigil from the blind. While I watched, the female finally returned and began to flutter hesitantly about the nest, alighting, flying off and then coming back. She tried repeatedly to feed the young birds, but they had again become chilled and unresponsive. At last she swallowed the food she had brought and flew off, evidently not knowing that they would have to absorb some warmth from her body before they could eat.

I now warmed the young birds as before. It was two o'clock when I went back to the blind once more. Soon afterward the female returned for a third time, this time without food, and after a few hesitant and awkward-looking attempts to cover her young, she wriggled into place on the nest and settled down to brood. An hour later she left the nest. Soon she was back with food, and after feeding one of the young birds she settled back onto the nest. By now they had recovered their normal reactions.

It was 3:30 when I began to set up the camera and lights, a piece at a time, whenever the female left the nest to forage. The reappearance of the strange objects caused a moment's recurrence of her old agitation. But just then the male appeared and fed the young without showing any noticeable anxiety. The female was brooding by now, and soon her mate had gone off and returned to feed her on the nest. At four o'clock I took my first picture that day; by seven, when I finally left, I had ten photographs.

Most birds are extraordinarily adaptable—a trait that becomes evident when they are being photographed. Once they have accepted the proximity of the camera to their nests—as they may do from the start without noticeable distress, or, on the other hand, only by degrees—they appear scarcely to notice subsequent additions of even a formidable amount of equipment, including tripods, flash lamps, humming power packs, electronic triggering devices, and not infrequently the photographer himself, within a few feet of the nest. Such proximity develops most often with the smallest birds—warblers, wrens, and so on—which behave less fearfully in the presence of intruders than medium-sized birds of the thrush and blackbird families.

To photograph birds that nest high in trees, it becomes necessary either to build a platform in the tree itself or to put up a tower beside it. I used the latter procedure to photograph cerulean warblers forty feet above the ground. They accepted the tower, the equipment on it, and my own presence with such unperturbed confidence that I could stroke the female as she brooded her young. For photographing birds whose nests have been built beyond reach of scaffolding, or where constructing a tower is not feasible, I hit upon another technique twenty years ago, not long after I first moved my family to New Mexico. I had found a Western tanager's nest in Pacheco Canyon on the western slope of the Sangre de Cristo Mountains—the first nest of its kind that I had come upon in the ponderosa pine zone that is typically favored by these birds. Up until then, all the others I had found had been in orchards at the lower limit of their habitat range, where the stress of an unusual environment made them difficult to photograph. This nest, however, was placed in a thick cluster of needles at the end of a branch more than thirty feet above the ground. To make matters especially difficult, the tree itself grew on the steep canyon side. The beautiful setting of the nest, and the male's mature nuptial plumage, made me all the more eager to photograph these birds—especially since both birds were actively feeding their young, as none of the others I had thus far discovered had been doing.

After considering all the difficulties that would be involved in building a tower, I was on the point of giving up the whole project when it occurred to me that the logical alternative to raising the camera to the height of the nest was to lower the nest within range of the camera. The more I mulled over this unorthodox idea, the more it began to appear entirely practical. A risk to the safety of the young birds was certainly involved, but I was confident that the risk could be minimized by meticulous planning and forethought. Above all, my knowledge of the adaptability of birds persuaded me that the scheme could be made to work.

My plan involved clamping a wooden bridle to the nest limb so that when the limb was cut off it would hang by a rope in its natural orientation, or could be quickly brought into balance in that position by the use of ropes. After this first critical step had been executed, and the adult birds had recovered from their initial agitation, I would proceed to lower the branch a foot or two at a time, allowing intervals between lowerings just long enough for the birds to adjust to the new position. Should they fail to adjust, I was prepared to raise the nest to its original location.

Even though I was without assistance, the operation went so well that it caused little disturbance to the tanagers. The first increment of lowering was the most critical. For an anxious moment, I watched breathless for signs of fatal confusion or of desertion by the adult birds. Had
I known then what I now do, I would have worried less. From the way birds react to artificial
situations of this kind, it is clear that they have a well-developed faculty for spatial orientation.
On their return to the tree after the first stage of lowering the branch, the tanagers flew to the
empty space formerly occupied by their nest and fluttered about in bewilderment, finally alighting
on a nearby branch to look over the situation. They behaved just as any of us would, I imagine,
were we to return home after a short absence to discover that the house had vanished: with dis-
may, some wild rushing about, and finally enough presence of mind to discover the house at
another location a few hundred yards away.

The tanagers soon found the nest at its lowered site and accepted it without further bewilderment. After each subsequent shift downward, they adjusted still more quickly to the new position, their innate concept of stability evidently revised to meet this unprecedented mobility. Within
an hour, when the branch had been brought down to a height convenient for photography, I had no
difficulty in taking all the pictures I wanted. I then raised the branch to a height where the nest
would be safe from ground predators. I revisited the site every day or so for a while afterward,
making sure that no mishap had occurred. None did, and the young birds fledged normally.

It should be emphasized that this technique is adaptable only to nests in evergreens whose
foliage does not wilt. Deciduous leaves wilt so rapidly that besides making natural photographs
impossible, the procedure means increased hazards for the birds themselves.

In my own experience, the maneuver has not been invariably successful. Thirteen years after
the experiment with the tanagers, an attempt in a situation requiring a modification was a partial
failure. This time the birds involved were ruby-crowned kinglets on Great Spruce Head Island,
off the coast of Maine. For days I had searched the upper branches of a grove of red and white
spruces near my house there for the nest I knew was hidden among them. The male had been
singing steadily for two weeks as he moved from treetop to treetop. Although he stayed high,
I had little trouble in locating him as he announced his whereabouts in a loud, often-repeated,
rollicking song. On the other hand, I had been able to catch only glimpses of his mate. I assumed
—rightly, as it later turned out—that she spent most of the time incubating her eggs, coming off
only occasionally to feed. I hoped to locate the nest by seeing her return to it following one of
these forays. When the eggs hatched, I would have a better chance to find the nest since both
birds would then be feeding the young. And so it turned out. One morning I saw them both
together, high up, flitting about excitedly; and as I watched I noted that their activities centered
around one particular treetop to which they repeatedly returned. Concentrating my attention on
this tree with the aid of binoculars, I was able to pinpoint a spot they both visited. It was a dense
clump of small branches some four feet below the top of a spindly white spruce fifty feet tall, surrounded at some distance by taller trees. Kinglet nests, consisting of a rather bulky pendent cup
woven from mosses, lined with feathers and attached to the drooping twigs of a spruce branch, are
usually very well concealed. This one was close to the main trunk of the tree.

As I considered the site, my first reaction was that the situation was hopeless from the standpoint of photography. The nest was so close to the trunk that the branch supporting it could not
be cut off and lowered without destroying its natural setting. The entire treetop would have to
be severed and lowered as I had once done with a spruce tree in New Mexico. But here no adja-
cent higher branch or tree from which to lower the sawed-off section was available Then I
recalled the experience in Minnesota of photographing a Cape May warbler's nest likewise built

BROWN CREEPER *Certhia familiaris* (Great Spruce Head Island, Maine: 1964)

WESTERN TANAGER ♂ *Piranga ludoviciana* (Little Tesuque Creek, New Mexico: 1957)

RUBY-CROWNED KINGLET ♂ *Regulus satrapa* (Santa Fe Basin, New Mexico: 1954)　　　　　27

AMERICAN REDSTART ♂ *Setophaga ruticilla* (Great Spruce Head Island, Maine: 1971)

BLUE-WINGED WARBLER ♀♂ *Vermivora pinus* (Battle Creek, Michigan: 1955)

YELLOW WARBLER ♂ *Dendroica petechia* (Great Spruce Head Island, Maine: 1971)

TRAILL'S FLYCATCHER *Empidonax traillii* (Great Spruce Head Island, Maine: 1963)

YELLOW-BELLIED FLYCATCHER *Empidonax flaviventris* (Ely, Minnesota: 1962)

WESTERN FLYCATCHER *Empidonax difficilis* (Pacheco Canyon, New Mexico: 1951)

WHITE-THROATED SPARROW ♂ *Zonotrichia albicollis* (Great Spruce Head Island, Maine: 1964)

CHIPPING SPARROW *Spizella passerina* (Great Spruce Head Island, Maine: 1971)

BLACK-AND-WHITE WARBLER ♀ *Mniotilta varia* (Great Spruce Head Island, Maine: 1971)

PARULA WARBLER ♂ *Parula americana* (Great Spruce Head Island, Maine: 1968)

CHESTNUT-SIDED WARBLER ♀♂ *Dendroica pensylvanica* (Seney, Michigan: 1955)

BLACKBURNIAN WARBLER ♂ *Dendroica fusca* (Great Spruce Head Island, Maine: 1968)

YELLOW-SHAFTED FLICKER ♀ *Colaptes auratus* (Great Spruce Head Island, Maine: 1968)

in thick foliage near the top of a black spruce—a smaller tree than this one, growing in a bog and at a distance from any other tree. To lower the top my companions and I cut a stout pole, which we stood against the tree and lashed to the bottom part of the trunk, and then rigged a rope sling extending from the upper part of the pole to the nest tree in such a way that when the nest tree was cut off above the lower lashings it could be lowered to a distance equivalent to the height of the remaining stump and re-secured in that position. By repeating this operation, the nest was gradually lowered to a convenient height for photography.

For the kinglets' nest a similar maneuver might be possible, I thought, except that for this larger, heavier tree the scheme of using a single pole would not work. I remembered a tripod frame that had been used the summer before to hoist large logs, and which seemed adaptable for my present purpose. It could be set up so as to enclose the tree, and from its peak a fall and tackle could be rigged to the trunk just above the place where it was to be sawed through. The top of the tree could be brought down to eye level, step by step, by suspending it from the top of the tripod and guying it to other trees. The plan seemed safe enough, and this time I had the help of the island caretaker. Once everything was ready, with all the lashings tight and a strain on the tackle so that the saw would not bind, we cut through the trunk. At first all went well: the severed tree remained straight and steady on its stump. To make the first lowering, the tree had to be hoisted clear of the stump and displaced sideways about ten inches. Just as we started this maneuver, a previously unnoticed weak point in one of the tripod legs cracked and then bent inward. Slowly the tree began to sway, and as the momentum increased it crashed to the ground, scraping past another tree as it fell. For a moment I stood aghast and petrified. Then I rushed to look at the fallen top, to learn the grim results of what I feared was a total disaster. I found the nest in disarray but still in place. It had been partly protected by the surrounding foliage as it sideswiped the other tree in its descent. But it was empty. On the mossy ground underneath the fallen treetop I found six naked young birds three or four days old. Four were alive and squirming, though one of these was bleeding. A fifth was alive but appeared to be severely injured, and the sixth was limp and motionless. I gathered them up into my handkerchief and placed them, handkerchief and all, in a bowl in the kitchen for warmth while I returned to the scene of the catastrophe to see what could be retrieved out of the situation.

The only hope for the survival of the young birds was to put them back into the nest after standing the tree up again—a formidable undertaking, and one that had to be done quickly before the adult birds deserted it. They were flying around in great distress, the male chirruping wildly, in and out of the empty space that not long since had been occupied by the tree. Fortunately, the persistence of their bewildered search saved the day. Goaded to the utmost exertion by their continued cries and scolding, we tried in vain to raise the tree with ropes and tackle; but it was too heavy for our equipment, so as a last resort we cut nine feet off its heavy lower end. Only then were we able to stand it up and secure it to the stump. I repaired the nest as best I could with thread and replaced in it the four surviving young birds, including the bleeding one; the fifth, severely injured one had died in the meantime.

Not without forebodings, I then sat back within sight to watch the kinglets' reaction and to discover whether they would be able to find their nest in its new location, fourteen feet below its original spot. Never before had I moved a nest so far from its original position in a single first step. For all my apprehension, I could not but marvel at the birds' unflagging perseverance. They flew back repeatedly to the point in space where their nest had been, fluttering and finding only emptiness. Then they would perch exhausted in a nearby tree to look the situation over before trying again. They would finally swallow the food they had been carrying for their missing young, fly off to gather more, and return only to be frustrated once again. Once the male alighted in the top of his own tree, and for a moment I was filled with hope; but he failed to recognize it as his territory and flew off without discovering the nest that was so near. One, two, three hours went by, and as my fear for the survival of the young birds grew, I concluded that there was no recourse but to raise the tree back to nearly its original position. Going in search of the caretaker, I found him painting his boat on the beach. When I had told him the story, he left his painting —which could not now be resumed until the next tide—to go with me, saying philosophically that first things must come first. He added with wry humor, "I have chopped down many trees, but I never before tried to put one up again."

He found three stronger poles, which he fashioned into a higher, sturdier tripod; then, with pulleys and rope, we raised the tree ten feet higher and braced it into position. When it was done, I stood back to see what the kinglets would do. The day was almost over now, and if this attempt to make amends did not succeed, nothing could save the lives of the young birds. While the tree was being raised the adults had disappeared; but after all was quiet again they soon returned, carrying food. They flew out into the space where they had vainly sought their nest for so long, found the treetop, and immediately disappeared into its branches. For several minutes great excitement prevailed as they rediscovered their offspring, settling down at last to the routine of feeding. They kept at it until dark, and that night I was much easier in my mind for having at least forestalled complete disaster.

The next day the caretaker and I completed lowering the treetop, three feet at a time, without further mishap. The birds accepted each successive drop without seeming to notice the change, until the nest was only six feet above the ground. They adapted to the new situation as though it had been planned that way from the beginning. I decided not to attempt any photography until the following day, so as to give the young birds more time to recuperate after their ordeal. The bleeding bird injured in the fall had recovered from its wounds.

Early in the morning of the second day, I went out to inspect the nest and found the kinglets flying in and out of it in a most unusual way for birds occupied with the care of their young. I saw at once that something had gone wrong during the night, and feared that the baby birds had died. But when I looked into the nest, I found it empty and torn open on one side. My first thought was that it had been robbed by a bluejay—and after all that had happened, the thought was almost too much to bear. Then, glancing down at the ground, I discovered all four of the young birds lying almost at my feet, alive and apparently none the worse for their fall. I gathered them up and held them in my hands to warm them; since they were quite active, I concluded that they could not have been exposed to the cold for long and must have dropped out of the nest only recently. Had that happened during the night, they would surely have died of exposure by now. The condition of the nest showed how inadequate my first efforts at repairing it had been. I could not put the young birds back as it was, since they would certainly soon fall out again; so, placing them once again in my handkerchief and the bowl in the kitchen, I went in search of something that could be used to make a more lasting repair than simply sewing up the friable moss. Finding no scrap of cloth for the purpose, I was about to tear up a handkerchief when I discovered a box of Kotex. Removing the cheesecloth from a pad, I folded it into a square to fit inside the nest, and sewed the moss to it with strong thread. Then I returned the young birds to their reconstructed home and sat down once again to observe how it was received by the adults. The male came first. As soon as he had peered into the nest, he began an excited chirping. The foreign material did not appeal at all to his sense of propriety, and he began to pull at it; but it was too securely sewn in to be easily removed. When the female arrived, she too attempted to pull away the cloth. I think its whiteness offended them, and the roughness of its structure may have been far less agreeable for their tender young than the downy feathers the parents had provided. But eventually they settled down to their domestic responsibilites, every now and then diverting their attention from them to give a tug at the coarse material.

The four surviving nestlings were successfully reared to the juvenile stage. I could not help feeling something akin to parental responsibility toward the family as I photographed them and watched over their day-to-day activities, seeing the young ones develop from naked quasi-reptilians to fluffy, bright-eyed, responsive baby birds. They became so accustomed to my presence that they showed no alarm when I stood beside the nest. When fledging took place—that traumatic matriculation into adulthood—I was there to watch. All four had left the cramped quarters of their battered home and were perched among the branches, loudly voicing their excitement as the parent birds appeared with food, and energetically exercising their little wings, which had blossomed out from the confining quills during the previous two days almost like flowers opening. The adult birds, sensing the young ones' need for encouragement, would refuse food to prod them into the maiden flight, that first great avian adventure. One by one they took off, heading straight for another tree at a distance that seemed to me remarkable on a first attempt, and landed clumsily among the branches. At last they were free and on their own.

Two Birds, like people, behave as individuals. They do not react automatically to either common or unusual situations, but respond in a broad variety of ways determined by past conditioning and experience. For example, although red-winged blackbirds have a reputation for preferring cattail marshes for their nesting colonies, they move to bushy pastures or alfalfa fields when the marshes are filled. Cliff swallows have readily accepted the shelter afforded by the eaves of New England buildings as a substitute for rocky cliffs. As an alternative to caves, barn swallows have become accustomed to nesting in farm buildings. Swifts now use chimneys in lieu of, and perhaps even in preference to, hollow trees. I once found a mountain bluebird, far from its usual haunts in the aspen forests of a higher altitude, occupying an abandoned gopher hole in the sandy bank of an arroyo. A redstart I observed shingled the outside of her nest with tiny scraps of white tissue paper in place of gray plant fibers.

In the summer of 1969 I discovered a nest built largely of twigs, cunningly concealed inside a curling sheet of birch bark a good eight feet from the ground. It was empty, and the builder was nowhere in evidence. I thought immediately that it must be a brown creeper, since this species invariably tucks its nest behind loose hanging bark. Moreover, brown creepers are known to work on their nests intermittently for several weeks before finally taking up residence. I kept the nest under observation, but never saw its owners and began to think it had been abandoned—until, one day two weeks after finding it, I felt inside and touched two eggs. Two days later I returned and gently tapped the covering bark to see whether an incubating bird would fly out. Immediately a small brown head appeared, far back in the shadow of the entrance, and then quickly withdrew—so quickly that I had no time to identify the bird I still supposed was a brown creeper. When I returned later in the day, no bird appeared in response to my tapping. Feeling inside the small hole, I found four eggs. To establish the owner's identity without a trace of doubt, I sat down nearby to watch for her return. After a short while, a winter wren appeared in a thicket near the nest tree. My mind was so set on the identification of the nesting bird as a brown creeper that I first thought the wren must have a nest not far away. I lost sight of her, only to see her reappear at the foot of the nest tree, make her way up a small spruce that grew beside the birch, and enter the nest. When I tapped the bark again, out popped the same brown head as before. How mistaken I had been! Here was a winter wren's nest made mostly of sticks. Could it be that she had adapted a brown creeper's nest for her own use?

These tiny wrens, the smallest of all North American birds except the hummingbirds, are reputed to be shy and furtive. That reputation, however, is less a product of natural secretiveness than of their preference for the thickets and boggy underbrush through which they move unperceived, close to the ground. A winter wren apprehended on its own terms, by patiently moving on hands and knees under fallen trunks and through tangled vegetation, is no less approachable than many other birds. It may then be observed in attitudes characteristic of all wrens. With its skimpy, reddish tail uptilted at such an angle that the bird seems almost unbalanced, it bobs restlessly about, chirring hoarsely, attending to no particular business other than scolding the invader of its privacy. When there are fledglings in the vicinity, they make their location known to the adults by a constant subdued chirping, which to human ears has a ventriloquial quality that makes the birds hard to find. The confusion is compounded by the dispersion of the brood throughout the undergrowth, so that their chirps never seem to come twice in succession from the same place. If one is lucky enough to spot a young bird, it turns out to be quite unafraid, and so approachable that it might be possible to capture by hand if one chose. Young wrens just out of the nest are fluffy, tailless mites who stare out at the world with the innocent, endearing expression typical of all baby birds. This impression of docile trust, however, is largely misleading. Fortunately, in most species the escape reaction is easily triggered. Not only can young wrens fly surprisingly well—as can other young birds—but they are equally agile in escaping capture on the ground when alarmed.

When young birds are not there to make their presence known, the movements of an adult winter wren can be elusive, and the nest itself may be impossible to find. No ground-nesting woodland bird conceals its nest more successfully. A few years ago, on Great Spruce Island off the coast of Maine, I spent many hours searching for the nest of a winter wren after I first noticed the bird—a brown, silent, mouselike creature moving about through a ground cover of skunk cabbage, low-hanging alder stems, and fallen branches. As it bobbed in and out of sight, its interest seemed to be concentrated on a brushy patch surrounding the upturned roots of a fallen tree. Knowing that winter wrens favor just such a habitat, I was ready to bet that the nest was there. Fortunately no one was near to bet with me. I knew just what to look for—a bunch of moss stuffed into a recess behind dangling roots, with no visible point of entry—but when I searched the place inch by inch, I found nothing. After this disappointment, I went back to my original position but saw nothing more that day.

Two days later I was back at the same spot. I had not been there long when I saw the wren flitting through the low, swampy vegetation. This time she was not silent, but gave voice to sporadic ticking and chirring notes; nor did she show any particular interest in the upturned stump. It occurred to me then that she might have been feeding fledglings in the brush on the previous day, and that they might now have scattered to a new location. I felt sure that if they were anywhere near, their continual chirping would have made their presence known to the parent birds. I watched while the wren worked her way warily around to the opposite side of me, grew silent, and then disappeared. Presently, after a wait, I saw her again, moving toward the base of a birch tree with a trunk six inches in diameter that stood not ten feet away from me. There she proceeded to drop onto a mossy mound and then to vanish before my eyes. I was incredulous. Could there be a nest in what seemed to me so unlikely a location? As I went over to investigate, the wren suddenly materialized again out of the forest floor, and flew off chattering. I had no doubt any more that the nest was there, but I still could not see it. Crouching to examine the mossy mound, which looked exactly like any moss-overgrown rock or mass of decaying wood, I found that it was soft and pillow-like to the touch, and that the moss stems of which it was composed did not stand upright as they would have if they had been growing there. Then I noticed that the moss had been wedged between diverging roots of the tree. Peering at the side of the mound, I discovered a small opening under a flap of moss stems, exactly at the level of the ground. When I put a finger inside, three young wrens burst out in rapid succession, chirring as they scattered into the woods. I had propelled them into the fledgling stage.

Two years later, drawn as a criminal is to the scene of the crime, I went back to the site and found the nest still in place, the opening now barely detectable and the interior hollow much reduced in size. The moss of which the nest had been so cleverly constructed had taken root, and was now alive and growing.

Another resident of Great Spruce Head Island whose nest I spent many hours searching in vain is the red-breasted nuthatch. This bird has never been abundant on the island, but is always present in small numbers. The name "red-breasted" is misleading—just how misleading I did not discover until recently, when I had the opportunity to photograph and observe the bird closely. In the one pair, I observed, at any rate, I found that the underplumage of the male was washed with a pale buff, running patchily from the throat to the undertail coverts but most noticeable on the flanks. On the female the buff color was still paler. Other characteristics were more useful in distinguishing the species from its white-breasted relative: its smaller size, the white stripe over the eye, and the weak, nasal call, higher pitched than the *yank yank* of the white-breasted nuthatch.

Over a number of years, during the spring and summer, I hunted in vain for the nest of a red-breasted nuthatch. Time and again I would find a pair of birds feeding together, chittering and *ank*-ing back and forth in what appears to be a habitual pattern of affectionate behavior. But I was never able to track them to a nest. They would invariably disappear into the thick spruce forest or fly off on a sudden impulse above the treetops. It was not until 1969 that I succeeded at last, and then only because of a fortunate concurrence of circumstances. That year I started looking in late May, before the birds could have begun nesting. Several pairs had already arrived on the island; I had seen them hopping along the branches of the larger trees, feeding and carrying on a steady flow of nuthatch conversation. On several different occasions I watched one pair in particular as they worked over a large white birch tree for dormant and newly metamorphosed insects. The tree seemed to have an especial attraction, for they returned to it again and again over the course of several days. Since the birch itself appeared to be healthy and free of dead wood, I ruled it out as a nest site. At frequent intervals the male bird would ingratiate himself with his companion by returning with a particularly succulent morsel, which he would place in her open bill. She would cease her own foraging as he approached, and with quivering wings and upraised head she would assume the juvenile begging posture. All the while, they would go on making chittery, conversational sounds. It was touching to see how the male did everything in his power to please her; feeding was only part of it. One day I came upon both birds exploring the cavities made by woodpeckers in the still upright trunk of a branchless, decaying balsam fir. They crept around the trunk, poking into each of five or six holes that had been excavated to a depth of no more than an inch or two into the trunk. One, however, was deep enough to conceal a small bird, and in it the male spent a long time excavating. He would disappear inside for a few seconds, reappear with a large chip in his bill, drop it outside, and then go back in for another. Eventually his mate came to make an inspection. Peering in, she bobbed her head a few times and flew off. Apparently the site had not been to her liking, for I never saw either of them there again.

A few days later I saw what I took to be the same pair, since they were in the same general locality, working on a dead birch stub about twenty feet tall, which had broken off at its base and fallen against a spruce tree growing a few feet away. Most of the bark had peeled away from the stub, and there were several shallow woodpecker holes near the top. In two of these, one about a foot above the other, the nuthatches were busily chipping wood from the interior, each bird hidden from view except for the tip of its tail. Every few seconds one or the other would emerge, back foremost, to drop the latest chip. The female alternated between the two holes, while the male bird worked intermittently on the upper one, flying off from time to time to forage and invariably returning with food which he would give to his mate before going back to work. She was much more persistent in this than he, and appeared to regard his comings and goings with a somewhat lofty and patronizing air. The two holes appeared to be of the same depth, and it was impossible to predict whether one or the other would be chosen as the nesting cavity. The habit of working on unfinished woodpecker holes, which goes on throughout the month of June, appears to be an abortive activity related to pair formation and courtship rather than to nest-building in itself. When I did ultimately find a nest, the diameter of the entrance was much smaller than any of these woodpecker cavities—a strong indication that the nuthatches themselves had been responsible for the entire excavation, and had not adapted a pre-existing cavity.

The discovery of a bird's nest often seems to happen just when it is least expected. I have many times come upon the nest of a particular species while I was concentrating on the search for one of another kind. Such unexpected discoveries are a reflection of the state of alertness that does not allow any sign of activity to go unnoticed. It was under such circumstances that I found the nuthatch nest—while I was actually hunting for magnolia warblers.

The date was July 3, and the setting was in the midst of a new growth of evergreen seedlings and young birches in a space opened by a blowdown a few years before. Most of the fallen trees had been cleared away for firewood soon after the storm that leveled them; but the survivors still remained standing in scattered clumps or as solitary mementoes of the forest that had disappeared. Tall, slender and branchless below a high evergreen crown, they held a precarious footing, one powerful gust of winter wind having deprived them of the collective support afforded by their neighbors. On this day in July, olive-sided flycatchers were announcing their proprietary rights—as they had been doing since early spring and every year since the blowdown occurred—with the persistent, whistled *peep-peep-peep* that is a sure sign that they are nesting. Since this bird prefers a lofty perch such as is left behind as the wreckage of a coniferous grove as a nesting habitat, the setting was ideal.

This natural clearing also contained a few gaunt, topless, broken trunks, forty or more feet tall, whose scaling bark still clung to the fungus-softened wood between the stubs of branches. While I stood waist deep in a tangle of young balsam firs and raspberry vines near one of these skeletons, I saw a small bird fly straight to it and alight near the top. Since a favored nesting site of brown creepers is under scaling bark, this was what I first thought of; but the action of the new arrival was unlike that species' habit of creeping up a tree trunk from below and then flying down. Having lost sight of the bird, whatever it was, until it suddenly flew away, I began to examine the trunk, foot by foot, through my binoculars, without finding any sign of a creeper's nest. The bird returned shortly, and this time I was able to keep it in view long enough to identify it as a red-breasted nuthatch and to note that it was carrying food. I watched it work its way down the tree until it reached a black spot that I had taken for a knot, where it paused; then I saw the striped head of a small gray bird appear and receive a morsel of food from the bill of the new arrival. Clearly the latter was a male nuthatch. Mistaking the other for a juvenile, I watched the feeding process for some time, wondering where the female was, and concluding that with the young so well grown, it would be hopeless to try any photography at this nest: the disturbance of setting up a scaffold for my camera would be sure to cause them to fledge. Then the bird inside the nest flew out and away without hesitation, and I saw that this was no juvenile but the female whose whereabouts I had been puzzling over. Clearly the breeding cycle was less advanced than I had supposed: the nest must contain either eggs or very small young.

Compared with the woodpecker cavities with which the nuthatches had been occupied in June, the entrance hole was much smaller than I had excepted. Another surprise was the nearly rectangular shape of the opening; those made by woodpeckers are almost perfectly circular. But what especially delighted me, coming as the first direct confirmation of a phenomenon well authenticated but not hitherto experienced in person—such as the first view through a telescope of the rings of Saturn, or the green flash at sunset, or the emergence of a moth from its cocoon—was the discovery that the bark around the hole was smeared with globules of pitch, with bits of dry grass and lichens clinging to them (probably as remnants of the nesting material the birds had brought to line the cavity).

After a few minutes' absence the female returned, without food, and entered the nest. Since she remained there, it now seemed most probable that she was incubating eggs. Meanwhile, with touching steadfastness the male bird went on providing her with a constant supply of food, no doubt as a continuation of his attentions during the courtship period.

The nest was at a height of twenty-eight feet above the ground. Since there were no trees near the stub, which was too shaky to be climbed, a tower would have to be built before the birds could be photographed. This I proceeded to do with the help of my son Stephen. We cut slender spruce trees for poles, using whatever scrap lumber we could scrounge as a platform for the equipment. When it was complete, the camera could be placed at the level of the nest hole, at a distance of three or four feet. The construction of the tower seemed to disturb the birds hardly at all, and when I sat on the platform on top to test their reaction to my presence so close to the nest, the male nuthatch took it in stride. In a remarkably short time he was feeding the female as though I did not exist. Setting up the camera, and especially the lights, called for another short period of adjustment; but these too were quickly accepted and then ignored. Except for the first two or three, all the photographs I took were made while I sat beside my camera. To test the reactions of the male when he returned with food, I once placed my hand over the hole—and found him trying to poke between my fingers. I took many pictures during the last part of the incubation period, and again after the eggs had hatched. But I never saw the young birds. My stay in Maine came to an end before they fledged. I concluded that like most other hole-nesters, they must stay in the nest longer than the young of most passerine birds.

Osprey (Great Spruce Head Island, Maine)—taking off

—landing with the wind

—landing against the wind

Arctic Tern (Matinicus Rock, Maine)

Arctic Tern (Matinicus Rock, Maine)

Common Tern and nest (Penobscot Bay, Maine)

Great Black-backed Gulls (Sloop Island, Maine)

56   Herring Gull (Sloop Island, Maine)

Three

The first group of small songbirds to attract my attention as a photographer and student of birds were the wood warblers. Finding them and their nests very early became a game that challenged my sleuthing skill and all the woodcraft I had absorbed during my school days. It began on Great Spruce Head Island, Maine, during the mid-1930s, and by the end of the decade I was keeping a record of what I saw and found. In the spring of 1938 I identified eighteen warblers; several of these were transients, but nine others I knew to be residents because I had found their nests. In later years this number grew to twelve confirmed species, with three or four presumed to nest, and the migrants bringing the total to twenty. The latest checklist of all nesting birds on Great Spruce Head and neighboring islands includes 66 species, and the total number recorded during the summer months is 95.

During those years of searching for nests on Great Spruce Head Island, I learned a good deal about the habits of some of the common warblers, their songs, scolding and alarm notes. I had discovered that certain species produced several versions of these. For example, the magnolia warbler utters a peculiar squeaky alarm note when disturbed by its nest; since it is not usually heard at any other time, it amounts to a sign that the bird is nesting and thus has led me to many nests. Another distinctive bird sound that I learned to recognize in Maine is the rasping scold note of the northern yellowthroat.

When I arrived in Maine on May 8, 1938—the earliest date in spring that I ever went there— the birch and alder buds were just beginning to open, and those on the spruces were still sealed in their brown papery caps. But the woods were buzzing with bird song, as the first wave of spring migrants began arriving on the Maine coast, two hundred miles from Massachusetts. Many of these were represented by both sexes—an indication that the males do not always arrive first to stake out breeding territories. Many individual birds were merely pausing to refuel after a night's flight across the Bay of Maine, before heading northward or fanning out over the mainland. Besides a number of blackpoll, blackburnian, and black-throated blue warblers, and a sizable representation of many other species, the majority were myrtle warblers, black-throated greens, and parulas. During those years, these three were among the commonest breeding birds on the island, and some of those I saw that morning would certainly stay to rear their broods. On that same morning I heard both variations of the black-throated green warbler's song—a fact that seems to bring into question the significance of a distinctive song in connection with breeding. It has been observed that the black-throated green male sings one pattern when near the nest or in the presence of the female, and another—with a more aggressive purpose —at the boundaries of his territory or in confrontation with another male. Unmated males have been heard singing only the latter variation.

A similar observation has been made concerning yellow and chestnut-sided warblers as well. In the presence of the female, both species sing a phrase accented at the end; as a territorial warning in the presence of another male of the same species, both sing a phrase without an end accent. Apparently many other warblers sing two or more distinctive songs, whose pattern is related to the reproductive process or to rivalry within or possibly between species. In Michigan, Betty Cottrille—with whom and her husband Powell I have spent many seasons studying and photographing birds in that state—has found that the blue-winged warbler during nesting produced a song different from the usual territorial song, and she used the observation to great advantage in locating their nests.

On Great Spruce Head Island during the late 1930s, one of the commonest breeding warblers was the American redstart. At that time birds of this species inhabited the alder swamps and birch groves in much larger numbers than they do now. I found many nests simply by searching the young alders within a short radius of the singing perches of the males. They were usually built in vertical crotches of the smaller alders, the common elder, and saplings of the paper-bark birch—quite low down in the latter two, and seldom more than ten feet high in the alders. The nesting materials varied considerably according to what was available nearby; although the nests all contained silvery-gray plant fibers in their outer structure, some had incorporated shreds of birch bark or used that material as a foundation. Near our boathouse on the island, female redstarts were seen to pull out fibers from frayed manila rope or to pick up scraps of cotton waste, a byproduct used in those days to wipe up grease around marine engines. I have already mentioned one redstart's nest which I found neatly plated on the outside with bits of white tissue paper. Deer hair and that of other animals, commonly used as material for nest linings by many birds, were not available on the island. Here, the lining consisted of grass, rootlets and occasionally a few feathers.

Singing in defense of a breeding territory is almost exclusively an attribute of the male bird. In some species, notably the grosbeaks, both sexes do sing; in still others, an occasional singing female has been noted. But these are exceptions. Before I knew all this, I had now and then observed what seemed to be female redstarts singing, and puzzled over why there were so few of them. What I did not know was that male redstarts acquire their full adult plumage only in the second year; during the first year, male adults closely resemble females. This became clear enough when I discovered a nesting pair of redstarts, both of which appeared at first sight to be females. On closer observation, I noted that one, although without the glossy black plumage of the fully mature male, was nevertheless considerably darker than the other, with brighter yellow on the tail and wings.

With changes in the vegetation of the island, the nesting behavior of the redstart population has likewise changed. As the alders that had taken over the wetter parts of cleared land grew to large size, spruces began to fill in the upland meadows and pastures, young birch copses matured, and as smaller trees were overshadowed and died the woods became more open and freer of tangled undergrowth. Fewer birds nested in the aging alders; instead, they chose the birch groves and mixed growth of birch and spruce. Similarly, as the sproutland seedlings grew up and the number of nesting sites in young trees diminished, more nesting birds chose the higher branches of the birches. In 1968 and 1969, and again in 1971, a majority of the nests I found were at a height above fifteen feet, and many could be found on limbs as high as thirty feet above the ground, in tall birches growing at the edge of a clearing or away from other trees. It also appeared that because of the changing habitat the number of breeding redstarts on the island had declined—although this observation may simply reflect the greater difficulty in finding nests higher above the ground.

On the other hand, the adaptation by the redstarts to changed nesting conditions has made it easier to observe the behavior of an incubating female than at the lower level, when the thicker foliage often cut off the view. So far as I have been able to observe, the incubation is done entirely by the female. During the thirteen days while she is thus occupied, she must leave the nest at frequent intervals to drink and forage for food. The male redstart does not always feed the female on the nest as is customary among other members of the parulidae family. When she leaves her eggs to search for food, she ranges rapidly through the open woods in the vicinity of the nest in the manner peculiar to an incubating female. She flits about nervously from branch to branch, picking up small insects and larvae from leaves and twigs, her tail fanned out and wings partly spread, continuously uttering sharp chipping sounds. It is these sounds that have frequently attracted my attention. The jerkiness of her flight, and the scolding notes, suggest an agitated attempt to focus the attention of a predator away from her vulnerable nest; and this is possibly the very purpose served by her actions. If she is kept in sight while thus engaged, which is never for very long, she can be followed back to the nest. Should one lose track of her, however, she can almost certainly be discovered again on a later feeding foray.

The parula warbler is unique among tree-nesting birds because of its nesting requirements. Its original breeding habitat appears to have been in the region of the Gulf of Mexico, where the trailing strands of an epiphytic plant commonly known as Spanish moss, found growing on live-oak trees, is used by warblers of this species to build their nests. With the withdrawal of the glaciers, the range of these birds spread gradually northward, and they discovered a comparable ecological niche in coniferous forests where the Usnea lichen or beard moss commonly grows. They use the strands of the lichen to construct pendent pouches among the clumps that festoon the spruce trees of northern forests, skillfully drawing the trailing filaments together underneath a branch to form a durable sack. No other material is used, except now and then a few spears of grass for the lining. It might be expected that these nests would be found only in dense growths of the lichen; but quite often the entire mass is used, without leaving anything over by way of camouflage. Nests constructed in this way are easily spotted from the ground.

The nests built by black-throated green warblers are rather large, deep, thick-walled cups with a variety of natural components, including plant fibers, moss, and twigs, with finer materials worked into the interior. The outside is beautifully decorated with curly, papery strips of birch bark. Hair and feathers when available, thin grass stems, rootlets, and moss spore stalks are molded into a lining by the female as she shapes the nest with her body, pressing the sides out and causing the thick rim to curl slightly inward. The cup is so deep that during incubation the only parts of the bird visible are the top of her head, with the bill pointing upward, on one side, and her tail on the other. Black-throated green warblers generally place their nests near the outer end of a branch in a spruce tree where the foliage is thickest, and where the branch immediately above forms a roof and helps conceal the nest from view. From underneath, however, such a nest is quite noticeable because of the fragments of white birch bark. It may be placed anywhere from a few feet to thirty or more above the ground. Occasionally one may be found built close to the stem of a seedling spruce.

The myrtle and blackburnian warblers also build their nests in spruce trees, placing them well out from the trunk among the smaller branches. The nests of the two species are in many ways similar. Both are loosely built of small twigs, lichen fibers, and grass, sketchily lined with rootlets, spore stalks, and a few feathers, and are much shallower and less compact than the nest of the black-throated green warbler. Myrtle warblers nest at a height of from fifteen to twenty feet, thus overlapping the height range of the black-throated green, but their foraging habits are said to be different. Blackburnian warblers choose a site forty feet or more above the ground, and do most of their food-gathering in the top branches of the same spruce trees. Field observers have suggested that the ecological niche occupied by blackburnian warblers may be defined by the height at which they forage, in addition to the parts of the foliage searched and their manner of doing it. Be that as it may, I found a blackburnian warbler's nest in Maine after I noticed both parents foraging near the ground and then watched them go to their nest high in a nearby tree. Conceivably they may be constrained by necessity to search for food over a larger territory while they are feeding their young.

The habitat of the magnolia warbler, another species of the genus *Dendroica* found in coniferous forests, is somewhat different from those just described. Magnolia warblers prefer the edges and cleared areas of the spruce forest, where young evergreens are growing up to replace older trees that have been cut or blown down. Their nests are always built fairly low in the wall of green branches spreading out into the light from the forest boundary, or close to the ground among the crowded seedlings of balsam and spruce that have sprung up in glades open to the sun. As you enter one of these miniature groves, pushing your way slowly through places where the growth is least dense, a squeaky, protesting note is a certain indication that a magnolia warbler has been frightened from her nest. A careful search, gently raising the top branches of the bushier seedlings, or merely the sight of a few projecting straws, may betray its location. The nest is a rather flimsy affair, consisting of a shallow depression on a foundation of dry grass and straw, with a lining of other, finer grasses. The golden spore stalks of cranebill and other mosses are arranged in a circle around the inside, intermixed with a woven layer of slender black rootlets which form the bottom. This structure seems to be the same wherever the magnolia warbler is a breeding resident. I have found nests exactly like this all the way from New England westward into the Upper Peninsula of Michigan and Quetico-Superior region of Minnesota, and northward from Lake Superior to Lake Nipigon in Ontario.

Much of my pursuit of birds in Michigan and Minnesota has been in the company of Powell and Betty Cottrille of Jackson, Michigan. Our friendship goes back to the spring of 1955, when we spent several weeks together near the Seney Federal Wildlife Reserve in the Upper Peninsula. I had gone there to photograph warblers in the company of Bill Dyer and Dr. Lawrence Walkinshaw, the noted specialist on sandhill cranes. It was with Larry Walkinshaw that I first visited the habitat of the Kirtland's warbler in central Michigan, as long ago as 1946 and 1947. He had shown me a nest of the Kirtland's warbler near Lovells, where I photographed the bird, as well as prairie warblers and clay-colored sparrows. My long association with Michigan began with an introduction from the National Audubon Society to Ed Brigham II in Battle Creek, where the Brighams took me into the family circle and introduced me to their friends among the ornithologists of the region. It was at this time that my interest in bird photography and my obsession with wood warblers were crystallized.

During the visit in 1955, we made our headquarters at a rustic lodge halfway between Seney and Grand Marais on Lake Superior. For three weeks we went out daily, regardless of the weather—and most of the time it was bad—to explore upland hardwood forests and black spruce bogs in search of nesting birds. Besides waterproof clothes and rubber boots, we wore head nets as a protection against blackflies. Walkinshaw and the Cottrilles were very good at finding nests in the rain, and on the few good days we divided up to photograph what we had found. Although Powell Cottrille always managed to display a nonchalant attitude toward our daily adventures and tribulations, the competition among the rest of us was intense, as though our very careers depended on finding more nests than anyone else. It was here that I obtained my first pictures of the Nashville and Western palm warblers.

In 1959 I persuaded the Cottrilles to join me for a month in southern Arizona to photograph Southwestern warblers. We met early in May at the Southwestern Research Station of the American Museum of Natural History on Cave Creek in the Chiricahua Mountains, where I had made arrangements for a month's stay. The birds we hoped to find were the red-faced warbler, the painted redstart, the olive warbler, and the Grace's warbler. Before I left the Research Station in June I had photographed them all, as well as three varieties of hummingbirds native to the Sonora Desert—the blue-throated, Rivoli's and violet-crowned. I had photographed birds in the desert around Tucson, Arizona in May and June of previous years; but for bird photography this trip was by far the most productive I had made to the Southwest.

After the success of the Chiricahua trip, the Cottrilles and I looked forward to working together again the following year. Aside from the pleasure our continued association gave me, the advantage was undeniably greater for me than for Betty and Powell since they outnumbered me two to one, not to mention their remarkable skill at finding nests. By now I had photographed thirty species of American warblers, or about half the total number found north of Mexico, and was wholeheartedly committed to photographing as many as I possibly could of the rest. Several that are common in southern Michigan were among them: the golden-winged warbler and its hybrids with the blue-winged species, and the cerulean warbler.

Finding and photographing a nesting cerulean warbler constitutes a special challenge. Its habitat is the upper branches and leafy crowns of broad-leafed deciduous trees in hardwood forests. Here these warblers sing, forage, and build their nests, seldom at a height of less than forty feet and often as high as sixty feet. Surrounded as they are by leaves, this height makes them hard to see and harder to follow; and even should one's persistence be rewarded, the discovery of a nest is only the beginning of an enormous amount of planning and effort before a camera can be placed near enough to make successful photography possible.

All these difficulties notwithstanding, we had decided that the reward of success would be great enough to justify almost any amount of time and effort, and so we agreed to go after cerulean warblers in the spring of 1960. I arrived at the Cottrilles' home in Jackson, Michigan, on May 20, and on the next day I found one of the sought-for warblers building a nest at about sixty feet above the ground in the oak woods not far from their house. The nest was saddled far out on a long horizontal branch, above a clear space in the woods with no branches or smaller trees below it. If this was a typical nesting site, our prospects were poor indeed, since the construction of a very high tower, a project calling for a considerable cost and great effort, would be necessary to photograph the birds that had chosen it.

So we decided to look for a more conveniently located nest, and in this we were extremely fortunate. On May 22, as we explored a small bird sanctuary near Jackson, we saw a cerulean warbler pulling bits of lichen from the trunk of a tree not more than fifteen feet above the ground. Knowing immediately what that meant, we froze our attention on the bird while she—for it appeared to be a female—continued pulling at the lichen for a few seconds more and then flew upward at an angle of about thirty degress. The steepness of her flight suggested that the nest she was building was not far away. Following the direction she had taken, we moved with suppressed excitement—and Powell was even able to assume an attitude of indifference—through the woods, each of us selecting a likely tree and proceeding to examine it carefully from the top downward for the warbler or any sign of a nest. We did not see the warbler herself until we went back to where we had first seen her. There she was, again pulling at the lichen. Once more she flew off in the same direction, and once more we followed her, focusing our attention on a large basswood tree that appeared to be in her line of flight. We were standing around the base of this tree, peering up through our binoculars, when Powell announced in a nonchalant, almost bored tone that he saw her and that she was on a nest. And once we had seen it, there could be no doubt about the nest—a gray, knotlike construction resembling that of a gnatcatcher, placed on a slightly upturned limb, not far out from the trunk of the tree, at a point where a tuft of broad new leaves had sprouted to form a sheltering canopy. We judged the height to be forty feet above the ground, and later measured it at forty-five.

We saw immediately that it would be quite possible to photograph the birds at this nest by setting up a tower at a height of not less than five feet below the level of the nest. After discussing ways and means, we decided to rent the requisite quantity of metal scaffolding from a contractor. During the days that followed, I leveled off a place on the ground where the tower was to be set up. Then there was nothing more to be done except to wait until the eggs had been laid and hatched. The laying would take four days, assuming the usual number and practice of laying on successive days. Although the incubation period for the cerulean warbler has never been precisely determined, we put it at about twelve or thirteen days, the period for other warblers of the same genus. Thus, allowing three more days for the completion of the nest and four days for egg-laying, with incubation beginning on May 29, and thirteen days more for hatching the eggs, plus two or three days more so as to give the young birds time to develop the strength necessary to withstand the extra exposure caused by our activities, we could expect to begin photographing around June 14. The scaffold could be set up two or three days before that.

With more than two weeks to devote to other birds, we located among us a large number of nests—those of a golden-winged and a blue-winged warbler, a chat, and a yellow warbler, as well as of an Acadian flycatcher, a short-billed marsh wren, a rose-breasted grosbeak, and many other common birds. The bird that interested me most was the golden-winged warbler, which I had found building a nest a day or two after Powell had found the cerulean. But the blue-winged warbler, which Betty discovered, was equally advanced and ready to photograph at the same time.

Meanwhile, Powell and I had set up all but the top section of the scaffolding by the cerulean warbler's nest. On June 12 we saw the adults carrying food and knew that the eggs had hatched, and on the next day we completed the scaffolding and set a platform of planks on top. As I stood there with my shoulders on a level with the nest, the female, after being frightened off by our activity, returned with food and settled over her young to brood as soon as they had been fed. When I reached over to find out how she would react to my hand, she didn't budge. Withdrawing, I watched for a while as she adjusted her position on the nest. Presently the male came and gave her a green caterpillar—which, after backing off onto the edge of the nest, she then fed to one of their young. All this seemed almost too good to be true. It would appear that unlike many ground-nesting species, the cerulean warbler has not been conditioned to react to the danger presented by large mammals, including human beings, and is therefore all but fearless when confronted with them.

It rained the next day, and the weather on June 14 was still unsettled—but not bad enough, I concluded, to rule out photography. Since the Cottrilles preferred to wait for better weather, I decided to have a go at it alone. Hauling my equipment onto the platform with a rope, I found that the warblers continued to go about their domestic affairs with little apparent concern. I made photographs intermittently between showers, and when the rain was too heavy I would cover up my camera and power packs with waterproof sheets until it was possible to go on. Although conditions were so unfavorable, I was able to take a number of pictures. While I was thus occupied, I noticed that although the nest was made of plant materials, including lichens, and possibly of spiderweb, which one would expect to become water-soaked and soggy, it was in fact impervious to water. Since lichens are known to change from a brittle to a flexible state after absorbing water, I expected the nest to be soft to the touch. To my surprise, I found that it was hard and stiff, as though cemented together on the outside with some impervious glue as the sticks that make up a chimney swift's nest are. Do cerulean warblers also produce a salivary secretion as a bonding material? It would seem that in their preferred site in the high forest canopy, on the exposed surface of a branch where no anchoring twigs are available, some kind of adhesive must be necessary to hold the nest in place against the dislodging effect of wind and rain.

We were all able to photograph the cerulean warblers several times. The last time I did so was on June 18, when the young were still several days from fledging. By then the peak of the nesting season for most southern Michigan warblers had passed, and we decided to pay another visit to Seney in the Upper Peninsula to try our luck with the later-nesting warblers there. We were spurred on by a report from the University of Michigan that Connecticut warblers were breeding in an area west of Marquette. If a nest could be found, it would be the first such record for the state—and Larry Walkinshaw, who with Bill Dyer joined us at Seney, was very eager to establish it.

After photographing black-throated blue, Nashville, and chestnut-sided warblers at Seney we departed for the area near Bruce's Crossing where we found Connecticut warblers, and Larry got his Michigan record. The nest contained well-feathered young ready to fledge; in another spot we found fledglings being fed by excited parents. Altogether, there were at least four and possibly six pairs of birds in the territory we searched—a section of dry, flat, logged-over land that was being reforested with poplars, maples, and saplings of other hardwood species. Because the birds were feeding young out of the nest, they were not difficult to locate and observe for long periods at a time. We quickly noted certain idiosyncrasies of behavior that distinguished them from most other warblers—the loud alarm note, more like a *whik* than the *chuck* of the ovenbirds belonging to the genus *Seiurus,* and a habit of walking along a branch or on the ground, also in the manner of the ovenbird, instead of hopping or flitting from place to place. The Connecticut warbler is less furtive than its congener the mourning warbler, staying more in the open instead of creeping about mouselike in the protection of thickets.

Two years later, in the bogs of northern Minnesota, we began to conclude that the Connecticut warbler was a much more common bird than the paucity of published sight and nesting records would indicate. We also discovered that it is at home in a habitat very different from the dry poplar ridges in southern Alberta where Taverner in 1926 had found it to be a common nesting species, or from the hardwood forest terrain of northern Michigan. We had already heard one singing in the Quetico-Superior region near Ely on June 25, 1961, the year before, and now we heard another in the same spruce and tamarack bog. This time the Connecticut warbler had top priority on our list of birds to be photographed. In almost every black spruce–tamarack bog we visited after mid-June, we would hear its characteristic song, whose loud and throaty character is not unlike that of the mourning warbler. As the days passed, however, the prospect of finding a nest appeared increasingly remote—until July 4, when the sound of a police whistle (we each carried one as a means of calling for assistance) brought Betty and me to where Powell was working alone. He had stirred up a Connecticut warbler, which was giving the loud *whik* we had become familiar with in Michigan. Soon we saw both birds of a pair, one of them carrying food. The male differs from the female in having a capelike hood of a slightly darker gray, though the difference is less distinctive than in the mourning warbler. The characteristic mark of the Connecticut warbler is an unbroken white eye ring—a feature not found in the mourning warbler, although a female of this species which I later photographed did have such a ring, faint but still distinct.

While we watched, the birds flew repeatedly, one after the other, to one of several small larch trees which were growing at wide intervals in the area. We were unable to keep continual track of both birds at once. Now and then one or the other would appear unexpectedly on a branch, walk toward the end, and stand looking down for minutes as birds do when they are preparing to take off from a perch. Eventually it would either fly to the ground and vanish into the bog vegetation, or fly off to another perch and go through the same performance. Once the bird had dropped to the ground, we would lose track of it entirely until it reappeared in one of the trees, scolding or carrying food. A careful search of all likely places for yards around the place where the bird had alighted in the bog got us nowhere, though we began to suspect that the behavior of the adults meant young birds scattered through the bog vegetation rather than a nest.

As the morning wore on, it began to rain and we were cold. Leaving Powell and me to keep watch, Betty went back to the cars for sandwiches and coffee. We had hardly started eating when without saying a word Powell stood up, walked about fifty feet to a hummock like the one he had been sitting on, separated the leaves and grass growing on it, and said with calculated indifference, "You don't have to look any farther. Here it is." He had noticed a slight movement among some blueberry leaves, without seeing a bird enter or leave the site. The nest he had found contained four young, well feathered and looking as though they might jump out at any moment. Standing back to observe the adults, we saw them creep through the tangled plants for a distance of many yards from the place where they dropped to the ground. Then, after feeding their young, they walked stealthily away again, sometimes as far as to one of the tamaracks, in which they would then perch once more.

The nest, beautifully concealed in a hollow in the hummock, was made visible only by parting the vegetation that covered it completely. Above the hollow grew a miniature blueberry bush; leatherleaf grew over one side, and the long, thin ribbons of sedge and marsh grass hung down over the other. A mound of mixed sphagnum and cranebill moss, curving out from under the nest, gave it still further protection. Laced through the moss were tiny, flat-leaved snowberry vines and the long, tough stems of lycopodium. More grasses—old brown blades together with the season's new growth—trailed out from the clump of moss. The nest, inside its mossy bed, was made entirely of dry grass. When the adult birds approached, they came through a tunnel of leatherleaf, grass, and Labrador tea.

By now the rain had settled down to a steady drizzle. All the same, I decided to try photographing the nest, since the young birds would clearly be leaving it soon. Two years ago in Michigan, the Cottrilles had obtained photographs of Connecticut warblers and I hadn't. Since they were not eager to try for pictures in the rain, I made the first try, using waterproof plastic to protect the camera and electronic components and working from a blind. The birds adjusted to the camera and lights very quickly, and were soon feeding their young normally. The bad weather had conferred an unforeseen advantage: it undoubtedly deterred the young from leaving the shelter of the nest, as sunny weather combined with the disturbance of human visitors would certainly have prompted them to do. This is just what happened the following day, when the weather improved and I returned to take more photographs: as the temperature rose and the vegetation dried off, the young birds became increasingly restless, and before noon they had left the nest. As it turned out, the pictures taken in the rain were the best of the lot.

In the meantime, we had become almost as eager to photograph the less rare but still more furtive member of the genus *Oporornis,* the mourning warbler. Birds of this species have a disquieting habit of deserting their nests if they are disturbed during the building stage or before the eggs are laid. We had already found two nests under construction and both had subsequently been deserted; so when Betty found a third, just finished, we stayed strictly away, keeping track of it only with field glasses from as far away as possible. It was not until after Betty and Powell had gone back to Jackson that I succeeded in photographing this bird. Because it was so late a breeder, I had stayed over an extra week for this purpose; but I managed to obtain photographs only of the female.

64

RED-EYED VIREO ♀♂ *Vireo olivaceus* (Ely, Minnesota: 1962)

MAGNOLIA WARBLER *Dendroica magnolia* (Great Spruce Head Island, Maine: 1945)

DOWNY WOODPECKER ♂ *Dendrocopos pubescens* (Great Spruce Head Island, Maine: 1949)   67

68   CANADA WARBLER ♀♂ *Wilsonia canadensis* (Great Spruce Head Island, Maine: 1971)

RED-BREASTED NUTHATCH ♂ *Sitta canadensis* (Great Spruce Head Island, Maine: 1971)

KIRTLAND'S WARBLER ♂ *Dendroica kirtlandii* (Luzerne, Michigan: 1947)

VERDIN ♀ *Auriparus flaviceps* (Tucson, Arizona: 1952)

ROADRUNNER *Geococcyx californianus* (San Xavier Indian Reservation, Arizona: 1952)

MOURNING DOVE *Zenaidura asiatica* (near Tucson, Arizona: 1958)

PAINTED REDSTART *Setophaga picta* (Chiricahua Mountains, Arizona: 1959)

OLIVE WARBLER ♀ *Peucedramus taeniatus* (Chiricahua Mountains, Arizona: 1959)

BLACK-CHINNED HUMMINGBIRD ♂ *Archilochus alexandri* (Tesuque, New Mexico: 1962)

RUFOUS HUMMINGBIRD *Selasphorus rufus* (Tesuque, New Mexico: 1956)

RED-FACED WARBLER ♀♂ *Cardellina rubrifrons* (Chiricahua Mountains, Arizona: 1959)

VERMILION FLYCATCHER ♀♂ *Pyrocephalus rubinus* (Rincon Mountains, Arizona: 1958)

BLACK-THROATED SPARROW *Amphispiza bilineata* (Tucson, Arizona: 1952)

In the summer of 1961, encouraged by our success in Michigan the year before, we had begun with a more ambitious expedition into Canada north of the Great Lakes, the heartland of the sub-boreal breeding warblers. We had our sights set on the Tennessee and Cape May warblers, whose breeding range extends from northern New England, Michigan, and Minnesota northward as far as Alaska. In the United States the nesting records of these species are few and widely scattered, and we had concluded that our best chance to find breeding birds would be in Canada. Starting out from Jackson on June 12, we crossed into Canada at Sault Sainte Marie and drove along the north shore of Lake Superior, through beautiful, wild, rocky country I found reminiscent of the coast of Maine. This part of Ontario was scarcely populated, the few settlements on Lake Superior depending for their existence largely on the pulpwood industry. To the northeast lay the broken, rock-ribbed land of the Canadian Shield, whose stunted spruce forest stretched uninterrupted for hundreds of miles. The only break in this vast wilderness was made by the thin steel ribbons of the trans-Canadian railroads.

On June 14 we reached Nipigon, where logs for pulpwood are floated southward on the Nipigon and Black Sturgeon rivers, which drain into Lake Superior. It was in the area around Nipigon that Charles Kendeigh had made a study of the relation between spruce budworm infestations and breeding bird populations, showing that the number of arboreal-nesting warblers increased wherever a plague of the insects occurred. According to the study, one of the commonest birds in the region, where a budworm outbreak had been rampant for several years, was the Cape May warbler.

We signed in at the Black Sturgeon River Lodge and set out to explore the region he had described. Since the region for hundreds of square miles was laced with logging roads, it was possible for us to cover a good deal of ground. Several years before, the spruce forest had been clear-cut for long distances in every direction, and poplar trees were springing up to replace it. With the cutting of the spruce trees, the budworm had been eliminated and the Cape May warblers, deprived of both food and habitat, had also gone. Obviously our search for this species was not going to be successful here. But there still remained the Tennessee warbler, and to look for it we shifted to swampy places that had not been disturbed by lumbering.

On our second day, we found in a black spruce–sphagnum bog a pair of Tennessee warblers whose behavior gave every indication that they must be nesting somewhere nearby. After following them around for several hours, Betty and Powell simultaneously spotted the nest. Sunk in the side of a mound of moss and woody shrubs, it contained five eggs. Despite this find, however, after another day's work in the field we had found so little in the way of nests that we decided reluctantly to leave Canada for the Quetico-Superior lake country in northern Minnesota.

At Pine Point Lodge near Ely, we were able to rent a cabin for a month. We soon discovered that birds of all kinds were everywhere, including all the common species of warblers. We concluded that their numbers were probably related to a budworm plague that had infested this part of Minnesota for several years—in some places so heavily that young balsams had been killed by complete defoliation. The larger trees appeared to be less vulnerable and to have suffered less damage by the insects. On inquiring, we learned that the Department of Agriculture had sprayed the forest with DDT in several past seasons but had finally given up in despair, leaving control of the plague to the birds.

By the end of our second day, we had explored a black spruce–tamarack bog and found three nests of Tennessee warblers, all containing eggs. The sites of all three were much the same: a sphagnum hummock or an old stump so overgrown with grasses, club moss, snowberry and twinflower vines as to be almost unrecognizable. Cape May warblers were also present in the bog, along with Nashville, myrtle, parula, and magnolia warblers, white-throated sparrows, cedar waxwings, boreal chickadees, winter wrens, and olive-sided flycatchers—to mention only some of the birds we saw in those first two days.

The principal difficulty we encountered in the bog was the swarms of mosquitoes and blackflies. They rose in such clouds that head nets were essential most of the time, making the use of binoculars awkward to say the least, and at times impossible. Mosquitoes can generally be discouraged by the use of repellants or reasonably impervious clothing; but not so the blackflies, of which the best thing that can be said is that they carry no disease. They emerge into adult life out of purity and beauty and would be destroyed by pollution of their larval environment. Blackflies start life as aquatic insects in the foaming, sparkling brooks found today only in the wilderness. When the larva is ready in June to trade its watery existence for the freer life of a fly, it builds around itself a sac of air and at the propitious moment lets go its attachments to the stone that holds it under water, and in this crystal sphere floats to the surface where the bubble bursts releasing at that instant its winged tenant.

In their search for blood necessary to insure the fertilization and development of subsequent generations of flies they exercise a determination and ingenuity for which they deserve the unmitigated loathing of all woodsmen. Liquid repellants and noxious ointments do little to deter them. To keep them from biting, trousers must be tucked into the tops of boots, jackets must be tight about the waist, zippers must be closed up to the chin, sleeve cuffs must be buttoned and covered by gauntleted gloves, and a broad-brimmed hat must be covered with a fine-mesh head net hanging well onto the shoulders and pinned to the jacket. Even thus attired, you may not escape being bitten.

A spruce bog on a sunny June day can be a sultry and oppressive place—especially for one wearing the recommended attire—but it is also beautiful. The trees stand singly or in small groups about its shrinking perimeter—mainly black spruce and larch, but with an occasional, taller white spruce. The billowy open surface of the bog is white with the blossoms of Laborador tea, which gives the impression of being by far the most abundant single plant—although leatherleaf and cottongrass, along with other woody bushes, are also numerous. In the early morning light, the dense white blossoms appear dazzling as frost, and the halo-like gleam of the low sunlight reflected by the needles of the spruces adds to the wintry visual impression. All this brilliance slowly subsides as the day advances, and the appearance of the bog becomes more commonplace. On the higher ground surrounding the bog, the trees of the mixed forest are larger and older, and the June air is perfumed by the thousands of pink twinflowers that carpet the forest floor, interspersed with the whiteness of bunchberry and wild lily of the valley.

It was in this setting that we finally tracked down the bird we were most eager to find. For several days we had been seeing Cape May warblers, but they had all been males and we kept losing track of them. Then, on June 25, Betty saw one carrying food. On the next day we also saw a bay-breasted warbler, but what excited us most was Betty's announcement that she had again seen a female Cape May warbler with food. We converged on the spot, and after two hours during which we noted and identified every bird that moved, Betty finally discovered the nest—only three and a half feet from the top of a twenty-foot black spruce, built close to the trunk. The unusual behavior of the Cape May warblers accounted for our failure to spot it sooner. They do not fly directly either to the nest or to the nest tree, but approach at a low level, usually going first to a nearby tree, then to the lower branches of the nest tree. They move stealthily upward, branch by branch, close to the trunk until they reach the level of the nest, then walk out onto the end of a branch to inspect the surroundings before going back to feed the young. On leaving the nest, the birds rarely fly out horizontally but instead dive for the ground before flying away. In the nest tree, Cape May warblers do not hop or jump, but walk on the branches in the manner of the Connecticut warblers we had observed in Michigan the year before. The female was much more timid and hesitant than the male in her approach to the nest, often waiting only a few feet from it for many minutes before getting up courage to feed her young. Now it was clear why these birds had been so difficult to follow after we saw them carrying food.

Using a ladder to climb to the nest, I found that it contained eight young birds about five days old, with their eyes open. The only possible way to photograph them appeared to be by lowering the tree, and we decided to begin the lowering immediately. Fortunately the nest tree was rather thin, with soft, weak branches, and thus not too heavy to manage easily. Cutting a gin pole and lashing it to the bottom of the tree, we ran a rope through a pulley at the top, halfway up the trunk, and then sawed through the trunk at about four feet above the ground, lowered the top and fastened it firmly both to the pole and to its own stump. The response of both birds to the maneuver was cautious. The female made one trip straight to the nest and fed the young. On her second visit, after a long interval, she landed below the nest, moved up part of the way, and then remained motionless for many minutes before flying out again. The male eventually came with food, climbed the tree in the usual way, and stayed on the nest. Late in the afternoon we left, hoping for the best.

Next morning we found both birds actively feeding the young. They now accepted the changes as we lowered the nest three feet at a time, cutting sections off the lower end of the trunk and shortening the pole to which it was tied at the same time, until we had brought the nest to a height of six feet above the ground. The female, however, still behaved somewhat more timidly than the male. Both adults were feeding the young mainly on budworms, although now and then the male brought a dragonfly. They came with their beaks full of worms—from four to six at once, to be distributed among several of their eight offspring. Clearly the budworm infestation was a bonanza for Cape May warblers in the area. As it was brought under control, the success of the birds in breeding would gradually decline, and in future years fewer Cape May warblers would return to the Minnesota bogs. Where they went would depend on food supplies elsewhere, and if they failed elsewhere the numbers of the species might diminish.

Our success in photographing two new warblers, the Cape May and the Tennessee, and the abundance of so many others, persuaded us to return to Minnesota the following year. I arrived on June 15, 1962, and when the Cottrilles joined me in Ely two days later, I had already found the nests of a Tennessee and a Canada warbler. Two days after that, we had found four more Tennessee warbler nests, two of them in the same sites as the year before—presumptive evidence that they were the same pairs. The number of nests we found altogether was still larger than the year before, and very soon we had a larger backlog of them than we could hope to photograph: yellow-bellied and least flycatchers, cedar waxwings, red-eyed vireos, white-throated sparrows, and several warblers including the Nashville and chestnut-sided.

A week after our arrival, we were back in our favorite spruce and tamarack bog, tracking down the Connecticut warbler, which we eventually photographed, when our attention was drawn by the high, sibilant buzz of a bay-breasted warbler. The bird was not far from where I stood, and we all saw him. It was Powell who followed him to a clump of black spruces and discovered the nest, ten feet up in a twelve-foot tree, with five eggs in it. Now our only worry was over predators that might destroy the nest before the eggs hatched to prevent us from taking our photographs. The eggs did hatch, and on July 6, when the young were three days old, I photographed them. With this done, the goal we had set had been accomplished.

But that was not all. Every season has its dividends. That year they included chestnut-sided, Canada, and yellow warblers, ovenbirds, red-eyed vireos, rose-breasted grosbeaks, phoebes, yellow-bellied flycatchers, veeries, and Swainson's thrushes, not to mention the female mourning warbler of which I succeeded in obtaining photographs that year after the Cottrilles had left. On my way home to Santa Fe I stopped off in Gold Hill, Colorado, where my son Jonathan was living, and spent several days photographing pileolated warblers that were nesting in an alpine meadow below Mt. Audubon in the Rockies.

In late May of 1963, I joined the Cottrilles in Cincinnati for a try at photographing such warblers as the hooded, Kentucky, and worm-eating, which nest in more southerly regions. Working in the Miami–White Water Ohio State Forest, where Ronald Austing, the well-known raptor photographer, is superintendent, we did find the first two species but not the last, although the birds were not uncommon in the area. The dividends that year were Louisiana water thrushes, wood thrushes, blue-gray gnatcatchers, yellow-breasted chats, and white-eyed vireos. Our failure to find a nest of the worm-eating warbler rankled so much that two years later we tried again (in 1964 I was in Baja California)—this time in southern Indiana, but again without success because we were too early. The birds were plentiful enough in the state forest where we worked, but while we were there during the second week in June they were just beginning to establish their territories and build their nests. Meanwhile, we had plans to go north to the Connecticut Lakes region of New Hampshire to photograph blackpoll warblers. A few years later, the Cottrilles visited Kanawha State Park near Charleston, West Virginia, still in search of nesting worm-eating warblers, and found fledglings but no nests. It was not until 1971, when I visited the same park in late May—having profited by their experience—that I found two nests and at last obtained photographs of the birds at both of them.

The Connecticut Lakes region, where I was able to photograph two blackpoll warblers' nests—one in a spiraea bush and the other in the more typical site, a spruce seedling—lies just below the Canadian border, where the Connecticut River rises. It is a region of clear trout streams, small lakes, and low hills deposited by the continental ice sheet. Birds of the Canadian zone are numerous here; besides the blackpoll, the Philadelpia vireo, and black-backed woodpeckers, for which the region is particularly noted among ornithologists, they include Wilson's, magnolia, black-throated green, Canada, and Nashville warblers, redstarts, Northern water thrushes, and yellowthroats.

Since moving my family permanently to New Mexico in 1946, I have come to know the birds of that state from the willow thickets of the Rio Grande and its tributary watercourses to the alpine meadows of the Sangre de Cristo range. In the juniper-piñon forest that covers the low foothills of that range, the only warbler to breed is the black-throated gray. In June this species is not uncommon there, and its buzzy song—similar in quality though not in pattern to that of the black-throated green warbler—may be heard as the males demarcate their respective breeding territories.

The black-throated gray and black-throated green warblers, together with the golden-cheeked, Townsend's, and hermit, are thought to have evolved from a common prototype during the advance and retreat of the Quaternary ice sheets, over a period of several hundred thousand years. It may have been then that the present migration patterns for many kinds of birds were first established—patterns that for some species continue to shift even to this day. The five species just mentioned all winter in Mexico and Central America north of the Isthmus of Panama. Their probable ancestor would have been a tropical species, as all members of the wood warbler family are by genetic origin.

At the beginning of the Pleistocene many of the wood warbler prototypes were presumably resident in the mixed deciduous-coniferous forests which covered the northern part of the continent late in the Pliocene. With the advance of the ice sheets the most northerly breeding individuals of these ancestral species could have been cut off by a wedge of the ice front from their more extensive breeding range to the south and east. Such a geographically separated group might then be the nucleus for the development of a distinct variant population. The migration of these birds, forced by the advancing ice into a new pattern, would, during the succeeding interglacial warming period, follow the advance northward of the forests to which they had become adapted in the western part of the continent, and thus remain geographically and ecologically isolated from the parent species. By a repetition of these events during successive cycles of Pleistocene glaciation several populations could thus have been split off from the ancestral stock. As interbreeding opportunities with the prototype species were geographically reduced or eliminated, independent evolutionary directions were opened for the isolated groups.

Of these populations, one emigrating to the northeast—New England, New York State, and the Great Lakes country—became the black-throated green warbler, while the one that is now the black-throated gray warbler traveled north into the montane coniferous and deciduous forests of the Rocky Mountains. A third group, the hermit warbler, spread westward to reach the Pacific and moved up the coast to Oregon and Washington, with the barrier of the Rockies blocking contact with the population to the east. A fourth population, the ancestor of the Townsend's warbler, eventually extended its range all the way northward to southern Alaska and the Yukon territory. The nesting ranges of the hermit and Townsend's warbler prototypes overlapped in the Pacific Northwest, where the present species now hybridize to a limited extent but maintain their distinct ecologically based identities. The last and smallest of the emigrating groups, the ancestors of the golden-cheeked warbler, extended their range only as far as the dry Edwards Plateau in Texas, where they adapted to an oak–cedar association not unlike the one inhabited by the black-throated gray warbler in New Mexico.

In pattern the plumages of the black-throated gray and Townsend's warblers are almost identical, the difference being that where the former is white the latter is yellow. The black auricular patch in these two species is reduced to an eye stripe in the black-throated green and golden-cheeked species, both of which are distinguished by having golden cheeks; but the crown and back feathers are greenish in the one and black in the other. The hermit warbler is like the black-throated gray except that it has an all-yellow head. All five species have black throats, and in all but the Townsend's the breast is white. These descriptions apply, of course, to the males of the species. A similar evolutionary process has been proposed to account for the differences between the myrtle warbler of the East and Audubon's warbler, its Western counterpart, which is found nesting in the spruce forest at altitudes of from nine to ten thousand feet in the Sangre de Cristo range of New Mexico.

Among the birds that find a favorable habitat in the relative humidity of New Mexico's dark mountain canyons is MacGillivray's warbler, the Western counterpart of the mourning warbler found in Minnesota, but distinguishable in having white eyelids—a feature most notable in the male. Building their nests in the wild currant bushes that border the ephemeral mountain brooks, warblers of this species are no less shy and secretive than their Midwestern relative. At higher altitudes, where the piñon–juniper forest is replaced by a mixed growth of Gambel's oaks and ponderosa pines, warblers of three species occur in limited numbers. The Virginia's and orange-crowned warblers nest on the ground in thickets where the oaks are most stunted, and Grace's warbler is found nesting in the pines. I have seen the latter more often than the other two but have never found its nest, whereas by a combination of luck and hard work I have found and photographed both the Virginia's and the orange-crowned species. Of these two the Virginia's is the more common; in fact, I have never seen more than one nesting pair of the orange-crowned warbler. To find their nest, I devoted the better part of a week after I first heard the male singing from the top branches of the tallest Gambel's oaks growing on a steep, gullied slope. For almost a quarter of a mile he ranged across the mountainside, staying always on the same contour, voicing his feeble trill repeatedly from the same high perches for minutes on end. Any of the singing posts, I knew, might be close to the nest, and I searched for it on hands and knees in the oak thickets. If I could flush the female, the search would be over, or nearly enough so that she would reveal herself by her scolding. Then, if only I could keep her in sight until her alarm subsided, she would inevitably reveal the location of her nest. Or so I thought; but the strategy proved futile. For hours, day after day, I watched the male from various vantage points as he moved about his territory, singing always from the same stations, but I never saw him joined by his mate. Soon nothing else mattered but to find that nest—to photograph this bird above all others became an obsession. Mentally recapitulating all the evidence for the probable locations of that nest in the territory over which the male bird roamed, I reappraised all my assumptions and started over again from the beginning. Finally, it was by adopting the hypothesis that what appeared to be his singing territory could not be synchronized with the breeding territory that my persistence was rewarded. Early one morning, a week after I had first heard the male singing, I wandered well beyond the boundary of the area he seemed to have outlined, and from across a small ravine I saw a small bird fly to the ground under a low flowering shrub. It did not fly up again, and while I pondered the meaning of this, the male orange-crowned warbler appeared on an oak close by. This time he did not sing; but presently the bird that had disappeared under the bush flew out and joined him. All but certain that here at last was the nest I had searched for so long, I crossed the ravine without haste—for I did not want to be too soon disappointed—and there it was: placed well underneath a buckthorn bush covered by clusters of small creamy blossoms, and surrounded by dried oak leaves. The five small eggs, wreathed at the larger end with speckles of brown and purple, were unmistakably those of a warbler.

My discovery of the nest of a Virginia's warbler, similarly placed under a seedling oak on the same hillside, took place in much the same way. This time I was looking down across a wide ravine when I saw a bird drop down from a pine tree into some low, scraggly oaks. I thought little of this until, as I continued to study the hillside, I saw the same thing happen again. An occurrence such as this is rarely by chance; so I focused my glasses on the oak clump, from which I soon saw a bird emerge—a gray warbler that could be nothing but a Virginia's. As I continued to watch, I saw her return a third time, carrying something in her bill. Now there could be no doubt that she was busy building a nest. As irresistible curiosity overcame my better judgment, at the risk of causing the bird to desert I crossed the ravine to investigate. When I found the barest beginnings of a nest, perhaps new that very day, I quickly retreated and did not return for a week. When I did so, I was relieved to find a completed nest containing eggs, which hatched in due course, followed by the successful rearing of the young.

Warblers that nest on the ground appear to be more secure than any others from predation by such larger birds as jays and grackles. This has been my observation, at any rate, on Great Spruce Head Island, where the most vulnerable of nesting warblers appear to be the magnolia warbler and the redstart. The nests of such species as the Canada and black and white warblers, on the other hand, seem to go undisturbed. Placed in a deep recess under a litter of fallen twigs, nestling among the roots of birch or maple, or sunk in a hillock of moss overspread with fern fronds, they are deeply cupped and constructed of materials that are scarcely visible in the undisturbed vegetation, and so well hidden as to be unnoticeable from even a foot or two away. The only hope of finding the nest of a black and white or Canada warbler is after seeing the parent birds go to the nest with food for their young, or the female returning to incubate her eggs after a brief foraging expedition. Such a nest cannot be found by simply searching the most likely location after spotting a singing male in a tree, as is possible with a species such as the redstart.

In the summer of 1971, while searching an alder bog for a redstart's nest in this manner, I became aware of the scarcely audible scolding by a mousy gray little bird. At first I mistook her for a female redstart, but after a more attentive scrutiny I realized that this was a female Canada warbler, and that she carried food in her bill—a certain indication that a nest containing young was hidden nearby. As stealthily as possible, I followed her movements through the alder thickets. But I lost track of her, and it was only after I had waited a long time without moving that she reappeared, once again with food—only to disappear once again without my seeing the direction she had taken. When the male appeared, also carrying food, I was able to see him drop down to the ground under a leaning spruce trunk, near the foot of a white birch thirty feet from where I stood. Certain that the nest was there, I went over to investigate; but a search all around and under the leaning trunk within a fairly wide radius revealed nothing. Just as I was about to return to my former point of observation, a bird flew out as I placed my hand on one of the birch roots. I had inadvertently flushed the female Canada warbler from her nest, where she had remained immobile all the while. Even then, I did not locate the nest immediately. Placed far back in a narrow crevice between smaller roots, it was so inconspicuous that at first I couldn't believe it was there. This is the kind of location safest from discovery by a predatory bird.

Four   For all my obsession with the wood warblers, I have not ignored other bird families. Among passerine species, the sparrows and flycatchers offer a special challenge to the photographer, of bringing out the subtle distinctions of marking and color by which they are differentiated. This is especially true of the sparrows, among which precise identification may hinge on gradations of color.

The flycatchers of the genus *Empidonax* present an even subtler problem, since the similarities are so great as to confuse a field observer unless their habits are taken into account. Until studies of breeding and nesting behavior, geographical distribution, song and call notes finally established a basis for distinguishing among them, taxonomists collecting and measuring specimens had debated the validity of specific and subspecific distinction among the Acadian, yellow-bellied, least, and Traill's or alder flycatcher of eastern North America. The dispute over the last, especially, went on for years. Was it a single species made up of closely related but geographically separated races, or was it in fact two species, genetically distinct and to be differentiated in their respective choice of habitat, nest construction, and song? Field observers had noted slight plumage variations, along with striking distinctions in behavior, between the Traill's or alder flycatcher of the Appalachian highlands, New England, the Canadian and boreal zones, and that inhabiting lower altitudes in the Midwestern and prairie states. The former, darker variety is associated with moist, boggy pastures and sproutland, where it builds a loosely constructed nest of dry grasses with many trailing stalks, very much like that of the song sparrow. It is usually placed low in the dense foliage of wild rose, spiraea, or raspberry bushes, or in a tangle of blackberry vines. The song of this flycatcher can be represented syllabically as *wee-bé-o*, and thus the bird is commonly referred to as the *wee-bé-o* type. The paler Traill's flycatcher of the more westerly lowlands prefers marshes or drier bushy fields, where the nest is built at a higher level than that of its relative, usually in an upright crotch of a dogwood, alder, elder, or willow, where it is less well concealed than the other. It is constructed of thistledown and gray plant fibers stripped from weed stalks, woven with dead twigs into a neater and more compact cup than that of its Eastern relative—one that suggests the nest of a redstart or yellow warbler. Its two-syllable song is represented syllabically as *fitz-bew*.

In the valley of central New York State, the ranges of the *wee-bé-o* and *fitz-bew* types overlap, and the two are found in close proximity. There is some evidence that interbreeding occurs here, producing offspring of an intermediate type whose nests and songs do not place them clearly in either category. It has been proposed that during the Wisconsin glaciation the prototype of Traill's flycatcher may have been split into two discrete populations, and that as the melting of the ice permitted both groups to spread northward, they were prevented from meeting by the developing coniferous forests, followed by those dominated by broad-leafed trees, that preempted the land vacated by the retreating ice sheet. As the forest cover was removed with the western advance of European settlement, this ecological barrier to the meeting of the two groups no longer kept them apart. Had the separation lasted longer, it is believed, the evolutionary path determined by environmental influence and mutational accident might have produced two distinct species.

Color photographs of the genus *Empidonax* clearly illustrate both the striking similarity and the subtle difference in the plumages of the species belonging to the group. For me, the most appealing is the yellow-bellied flycatcher, with its subtle gradations of yellow in the under plumage. It is a summer inhabitant of the dark, damp coniferous forests and the sphagnum bogs of the Canadian zone from Maine to Minnesota, where the trees are mainly alder and black spruce. This bird and its close analogue, the Western flycatcher, are the only members of the family to

Red-legged Kittiwakes (Bonaventure Island, Canada)

Gannets (Bonaventure Island, Canada)

Cormorants and nests. (Colt's Head Island, Maine)

Spotted Sandpiper
(Great Spruce Head Island, Maine)

Upland Plover (Lovells, Michigan)

94

Eider's nest (Sloop Island, Maine)

Snowy Egret (Kissimmee Prairie, Florida)

build their nests on the ground. I have never seen the nest of a yellow-bellied flycatcher in the open. It seems to prefer the shade of young spruces or an overstory of alder in the wooded part of a bog. The first such nest I ever found was on Great Spruce Head Island, sunk in a mound of moss at the base of a spruce tree. All the others I have seen were in northern New Hampshire, Michigan, and Minnesota—and it was that past master, Dr. Powell Cottrille, who found them. His affection for these flycatchers is even greater than mine, and he can scarcely resist tracking down their nests even when he has no intention of photographing them. The beauty of the setting these birds seem inevitably to select makes his enthusiasm easy to share. Usually they choose a hollow in the side of a moss-covered hummock, where the concealment offered by hanging leafy stems renders the female, nestled down on her eggs, nearly invisible even on close inspection and when the precise location of the nest is known. Her unblinking black eye and wide bill are all that can be seen above the narrow rim of grasses composing the only visible part of the nest. But bryophytes are not the only reason for the mystery of these hidden sites. The slender spears of grass arching over the mound and projecting between the leafy thalli of sphagnum or cranebill moss are a tremulous further addition to the camouflage, and such sturdier foliage as the lacy, drooping fronds of the spinulose fern, the trefoils of wood sorrel, along with leather-leaf, clintonia, maianthemum, and miniature snowberry vines, combine to produce the delicate unity of a microcosm.

This gentle, secretive flycatcher arrives on its breeding grounds in late May or June and departs once more for the tropics in August. But although its stay in the North is so brief, nearly everything that is known about its life and habits has been obtained during this period. Thus we know it entirely as a bird whose habits are uniquely adapted to the tightly circumscribed ecological system in the swampy woodlands where it breeds. It stays close to the forest floor where it builds its nest and rears its brood, seldom if ever deserting this habitat to explore the upper levels of the forest. Through this damp environment it moves like a ghost, flitting mothlike from one low perch to another, pausing to snap up small insects with a faint click of its bill and then darting on again. But its travels are not totally silent, and herein lies the secret of tracking down its nest. By patient watching and listening in its blackfly and mosquito-infested haunts, Powell Cottrille learned that the female flycatcher utters a characteristic couplet, not identical with the song of the male, during the brief intervals when she leaves her nest unattended in her search for food. The male's more incisive song is variously rendered as consisting of two or possibly three notes, with the accent on either the first or the second syllable, thus: *chú-wee* or *pee-weép.* The female's couplet, which Powell refers to as the nest song, is a softer, more drawn-out, plaintive *peee-weee,* without an accent, produced at frequent intervals. It has a sweet, sad quality, and Powell says it is a certain indication of a nest hidden in the vicinity. Once the author of the song has been found, if she can be kept in sight as one discreetly follows her through the lower-story vegetation, she will lead one to her nest—a theory that is simple enough, though in practice keeping track of a small, well-camouflaged bird in the leafy environment of a sphagnum bog is something else again.

The yellow-bellied flycatcher's Western counterpart inhabits moist canyon bottoms in northern New Mexico, and I have found it there in considerable numbers. The plumage of the Western flycatcher's breast and belly is paler than that of the yellow-bellied, and although in some respects its nesting habits are analogous, there are also some striking differences. It finds a suitable habitat in Pacheco Canyon, on the western slope of the Sangre de Cristo Mountains a few miles north of Santa Fe, at an elevation of about eight thousand feet. For a considerable distance the canyon is narrow and shaded, supporting a mixed vegetation of streamside willows, wild currant, aspens, ponderosa pines, white and Douglas firs. The firs thrive in the dark, wet bottom of the canyon, whereas the pines also grow along the drier sides, intermingling at the tops of ridges with scattered junipers and Gambel's oaks. It is in the canyon bottom that the Western flycatcher nests, along with MacGillivray's warblers, Audubon's hermit thrushes, house wrens, red-naped and Williamson's sapsuckers. I have found their nests in varied situations, the most usual being on a narrow ledge of a steep bank, in a cover of moss; but besides rotting stumps several feet above the ground, the sites have included, most unexpectedly, the joists under bridges—a spot commonly chosen by phoebes.

Two other *Empidonax* flycatchers occur in and around Pacheco Canyon. The Hammond's builds its nest high in the branches of the tallest pines and firs growing on the canyon floor. The preferred habitat of the Wright's flycatcher, also known as the dusky flycatcher, is the thickets of Gambel's oak on the dry slopes and ridges above the canyon. The nests of this species are constructed of plant down and fibers in a neat, compact cup attached to the forked oak branches, rarely more than five feet above the ground. They look like the nests of the *fitz-bew* Traill's flycatcher or of the black-throated gray warbler, whose chosen habitat is the piñon–juniper association of a lower altitude. Associated with the Wright's flycatcher on these oak ridges are spotted and green-tailed towhees, Virginia's and orange-crowned warblers—all ground nesters—along with black-headed grosbeaks in the oak trees, and Western tanagers and Steller's jays in the ponderosa pines.

The member of the genus *Empidonax* commonly called the Acadian flycatcher is misnamed, owing to the erroneous designation of a specimen taken in Nova Scotia (Acadia) as the type of the species. It was later established that the specimen was actually a Traill's flycatcher, and that the so-called Acadian species never reaches Nova Scotia. Its habitat is in the broad-leafed deciduous forest of the Midwest and South. It is found nesting only where a high forest crown produces a condition of discontinuous light and shade unlike the continual gloom of the tropics, one where the seedlings of shade-tolerant dogwoods and trees of the climax growth find a favorable balance. The scientific name *Empidonax virescens* (given to the species after the error in the type specimen was discovered in place of *acadicus,* though the common name continues in use as before) is appropriate, since its plumage is greener than any other in the group. Nevertheless, to identify the Acadian flycatcher in the field by sight alone is all but impossible unless the song, habitat, and nest structure are verified. This is the only flycatcher of the genus commonly found in the woodland conditions just described, whereas the Traill's requires bushy open country, pastureland, or alder swamps, and the yellow-bellied is found only in the bogs of the coniferous forest. The nest of the Acadian flycatcher is usually built at a height of less than fifteen feet in the shrubbery of the forest understory, placed in a horizontal fork of a small dogwood tree or a sapling of the principal climax species. It consists of a shallow, pendent cup, woven of plant fibers and grasses and suspended in the manner of a vireo's at the junction of the two branches. It is a frail structure compared with the vireo's, however: the mesh is so open that the eggs can be seen through it from below, and the fabric as a whole is so unsubstantial that it rarely lasts through the winter—unlike the vireo's nest, which may survive disintegration for several seasons.

The altitudinal range of habitats near my home in New Mexico has made possible a great diversity of bird species within a rather circumscribed geographical area. Thus, in the grassland of the valleys and along the course of the Rio Grande, where the Conquistadors found grass tall enough to brush the bellies of their horses, but where after centuries of overgrazing it grows no more than a few inches high, such ground-nesting birds as horned larks, lark sparrows, and Western meadowlarks are to be found. Among the evergreens of the piñon–juniper association, where the trees are dwarfed and widely spaced, the nesting birds include white-rumped shrikes and mockingbirds, as well as such occasional wanderers as the black-throated desert sparrow and other Lower Sonoran species.

At a somewhat higher altitude, where the junipers and piñons are denser, piñon jays nest in loose colonies. These gregarious birds regulate their nesting with the availability of their staple food, the seeds of the piñon pine. In years when the production of piñon nuts is poor, they may not breed at all, or nesting may abort after a tentative beginning. Nesting may occur at almost any time except during the coldest months of the winter. Following an abundant crop of piñon nuts in the fall, the jays may begin building their nests in March, and they may do so as late as October. In April, 1948, I found twenty piñon jay nests on a ridge just south of the Santa Fe city limits. The colony had been pointed out to me by my friend Jens Jensen, an amateur ornithologist living in Santa Fe, who had also discovered more nests in another area about a mile farther south on the same ridge. Young birds were successfully raised in only three of the twenty-six nests. The causes of the high degree of failure were complex. Eight of the nests had been deserted before or just after completion, possibly because the supply of piñon nuts was inadequate. Eggs were laid in the remaining nests—only one or two in some, although the majority contained a full clutch of four. Broken shells and disturbed nest linings found in many of these, and scraps of skin and fur in one, suggested that there had been predation by ground squirrels—although squirrels could not necessarily be blamed for the disappearance of eggs from nests which otherwise showed no sign of having been plundered. The mystery was compounded by the discovery of one nest on which the incubating female lay dead above her eggs. It occurred to me that poisons put out to kill rodents might have destroyed the colony.

It was at one of these colonies that I photographed piñon jays and witnessed some of their peculiar habits. The birds adjusted quickly to the presence of the photographic equipment, showing signs of uneasiness only when it was necessary for me to change the film. During the first two days of photographing them, the weather was cool even though it was mid-May, and since the young were still without feathers, the female stayed on the nest to brood for long periods. From time to time she would rise up on the nest and feed her young by regurgitation, and when her mate appeared he too fed them in this manner. Sometimes she would assist by taking some of the food he had raised from his crop and giving it to the young birds. She kept the nest scrupulously clean by swallowing all her young's excrement, and in every respect was a most devoted and solicitous parent. When I changed the film in the camera, she would quietly slip off the nest, to return as soon as I went back to my car, from which I operated the remote-control switch.

Feeding by regurgitation is not practiced by scrub jays or by the Eastern bluejay, but is the method used by crows. I first watched this manner of feeding in Maine, from a blind in a spruce tree containing a crow's nest, and the similarity of this habit to that of the piñon jays led me to recognize a closer relationship between the two than between the piñon and other jays. The Spanish-American people of New Mexico have long called the piñon jays blue crows—one more illustration of the perspicacity of country folk whose understanding of nature is based not on books but on direct observation. Whether piñon jays share a propensity for polygamy or polyandry with crows I do not know, but I should be less than surprised if they did.

The piñon–juniper flats frequented by piñon jays are also the habitat of the gray vireo, the gray flycatcher, and the Western gnatcatcher, a drab version of the blue-gray gnatcatcher found in the East. Birds of this species are immediately recognizable by their small size and longish tails, their sizzling voices and continual nervous activity. A pair in the act of building a nest may seem to be completely preoccupied and indifferent to observation; but it is well not to approach them too closely or to linger watching them at work, since they have the odd habit of moving their nests as soon as the observer has gone, provided no eggs have been laid. I remember once coming across a busy and vocal couple, one member of which carried an enormous beakful of nesting material that looked like cotton lint. I watched them only long enough to find out where the nest was being built, and then left immediately. After allowing time for the nest to be completed and for the female to lay a full clutch of eggs, I returned to find no trace of the nest—not a scrap of material or any indication that a nest had ever been started. It and the birds themselves had vanished so completely that I almost doubted the soundness of my memory.

In this same dry forest zone two species, the brown or canyon and the spotted or rufous-sided towhee, live the year round in an environment that changes only with seasonal cycle. In winter they forage for the seeds of wild grass and for those of the chamise, which sift to the ground from thickets of pale golden plumes. When snow blankets the ground and the seeds are hard to find, sub-zero temperatures send them to my feeder; but with the advent of warm weather, they retreat once again to the safety of the chamise thickets to nest, the spotted towhee on the ground while the canyon towhee builds a bulkier structure among the protective branches. In other respects their habits are not at all similar. Except in its nesting behavior, the spotted towhee is far less secretive than the brown or canyon towhee, which skulks through the underbrush and utters a mewing, metallic complaint when disturbed. The song of the latter bird is a monotonous series of notes, all on one pitch, like the rattle of the chipping sparrow but of greater volume. The song of the spotted or rufous-sided towhee is cheerier, resembling that of its relative the Eastern red-eyed towhee, and the male sings indefatigably from the first warm day of March until well into July.

In the shaded canyons above the piñon–juniper zone, ribbons of the forests of fir, ponderosa pine, and aspen that grow at higher altitudes extend downward, cutting through the expanse of sun-baked slopes. Here, in addition to the MacGillivray's warbler and the Hammond's and Western flycatchers, the nesting birds include the red-naped and Williamson's sapsuckers, which drill their nest holes in living aspens, and the violet-green swallow, whose preferred nesting site is in old sapsucker holes, with hollow trees a second choice. Still another canyon resident is the Audubon's hermit thrush, which builds a bulky nest in a seedling fir rather than on the ground like its Eastern relative.

As one ascends these canyons, the mountain slopes on either side become less precipitous, and Gambel's oaks and ponderosa pines replace the piñons and junipers. The oaks on these open slopes rarely grow more than ten feet high, in low, scrubby tangles that form a lower-story vegetation among the pines. Here black-headed grosbeaks and Wright's or dusky flycatchers are the common residents of the oak thickets, and where the oaks are small and scattered they give cover for such ground-nesting birds as gray-headed juncos, the spotted or rufous-sided towhee, and—at the lower limit of their range—the green-tailed towhee. These slopes are also the home of the Virginia's, orange-crowned, and Grace's warblers. But the commonest breeding birds of the ponderosa pine–Gambel's oak association are the Western tanager and the Steller's jay. For nesting the jay appears to prefer young Douglas firs growing in cool, sheltered draws already partly pre-empted by aspens. Tanagers nest in the more mature pines and firs, well out toward the end of a branch where the foliage is thickest. My first experience in photographing a nest by lowering it has already been described. Another time, I used the same technique to lower a tanager's nest containing downy young. The female had accepted the new position although the male had not, and I had begun photographing her when a sudden rainstorm rapidly turned into a cloudburst, accompanied by hail. The female now disappeared, probably in search of shelter, and her forsaken young were soon soaked and in danger of being killed by the hailstones. Removing them to the shelter of my car, I dried them off and warmed them under the heater. After the storm had passed I returned them, dry and lively, to their nest before the mother returned to carry on her interrupted maternal duties as though nothing had happened.

As one moves upward in the Sangre de Cristo range, the Douglas firs become more numerous, replacing the ponderosa pines until at an altitude between nine and ten thousand feet the forest consists mainly of spruce and fir, with stunted aspens occupying slopes swept by fire in years past. With this change in vegetation, the bird life is likewise modified. A few species found at lower altitudes, such as house wrens, gray-headed juncos, and green-tailed towhees, are more abundant here. So are the Audubon's warbler and Audubon's hermit thrush. And as the climate becomes the equivalent of that prevailing in the damp evergreen forests of Canada, many species known otherwise only to more northerly latitudes appear. Among the most common is the ruby-crowned kinglet, quickly recognizable by its bubbling song, and trailed without much difficulty to its nest in the thick upper foliage of the spruce trees, which grow in parklike natural stands. Pine siskins, which likewise prefer the spruces, are also abundant. Among the wild currant bushes that flourish in the high valleys where the soil is too wet for evergreens, and along the mountain brooks, the white-crowned sparrow nests along with the green-tailed towhee. The white-crowned sparrow's plaintive, lisping whistle as it announces its territorial boundary is the same sound—or so it would seem—as may be heard on winter evenings among the willow thickets lining the irrigation ditches at a lower altitude. But the birds are not the same; the winter residents are Gambel's white-crowned sparrows, and their breeding grounds lie far to the north. The one visible difference between the two races is in the eye stripe, which in the Gambel's white-crowned sparrow starts at the bill rather than at the eye as in the race that breeds in the Sangre de Cristos and migrates farther south for the winter.

Gray jays, the camp robbers of the Rocky Mountains, roam the spruce forests, giving their whining call, along with Clark's nutcrackers, which here reach the southernmost limits of their range. In July and August, the males of two species of hummingbirds, the rufous and calliope, on their way southward from nesting territories in British Columbia and Alaska, rattle from blossom to blossom of the Indian paintbrush.

In these high alpine basins, the spruce trees stand on ground slightly higher than the open meadow, where such disparate elements as the milky-plumed hellebore, with its fans of stiff, accordion-pleated leaves, and the drooping, fragile, blue-pink clusters of the mertensia are part of a synthesis that is at once harmonious and marvelously complex, the undisturbed creation of a multiplicity of forces that have been at work here for perhaps ten thousand years. It was in such a setting that I discovered my first ruby-crowned kinglet's nest. While I sat looking down on the meadow and the serrated profile of a grove of spruces, I became aware of a small bird flying repeatedly into the top of one of the shorter trees, and identified it as a kinglet. Since its behavior suggested the presence of a nest, I climbed the tree and found one still in the process of being built. After the eggs had hatched, I was able to photograph the birds by roping the top of the nest tree to a taller neighbor, cutting it off, and then lowering it gradually to the ground between the two trees. The kinglets proved remarkably adaptable to their changed situation, and I was able to carry on my photographic activities from only a dozen feet away. Once I had finished, I hoisted the cut-off top to about half its original height and left it there until after the young birds had flown. Although at first glance the situation had not promised such easy success, it was one of the simplest nest-lowering projects I ever undertook.

Higher yet on the mountainside under the crumbling rock walls of glacial cirques, in which the last remnants of Pleistocene ice melted thousands of years ago, the frigid waters of small tarns retain through the short alpine summer a continuity with the blue ancestral ice that produced and fed them. The rock amphitheaters nearby are the summer haunts of western ravens who—following the serious business of bringing up their young—play wild unrestrained acrobatic games in the up-rushing drafts above the perpendicular cliffs that echo their frenzied croaks. From the stunted shrubbery and sphagnum hummocks that choke the marshy outlet of the tarn, the sweet song of the Lincoln's sparrow acts as counterpoint to the harsh cries of the ravens.

On the treeless crests of the highest peaks, where summer begins in July and ends in August, the vegetation becomes subarctic. Scattered along the Rocky Mountain range all the way to Canada, these tundra—like areas ultimately coalesce at a lower altitude with the Hudsonian zone of vegetation. Here, as in the arctic, fully mature willow trees are only six inches high, and the flowering plants include saxifrages, gentians, alpine primroses and phlox, and sky-blue dwarf forget-me-nots. Two species of birds nest in these arctic barrens: the Townsend's solitaire, which migrates vertically from its winter home in the river valleys at the end of June, when mountains have shed their mantles of snow, and the American pipit, a genuinely arctic species, whose range stretches across the Western hemisphere from southern Greenland and northern Labrador to the northern coast of Alaska, and some of whose races have retained a foothold on these mountaintop outposts of the ice age as far south as New Mexico. Both the solitaire and the pipit nest in sheltered nooks under logs or slabs of rock, or in sod banks that offer some concealment from the searching eyes of gray jays and nutcrackers.

In September, when the birds begin to come down from the mountains, my wife and I walk out each morning into the piñon—juniper region behind our house to watch for them and to look for wildflowers. After a wet August, flowers spring up everywhere as in a second spring, and as in spring the birds are singing. One call, a single, sweet, clear, flutelike note, sounds again and again. After spending the summer on Great Spruce Head Island, it is no longer familiar. And if I do not remember the note, neither can I find the bird, blinded as I am by the sunrise over the western foothills of the Sangre de Cristo range. From the top branches of the low piñons and junipers, other birds answer the call; but their silhouettes are indistinguishable from the bushy outlines of the trees in the sharp morning light. Then, as one begins a soft, melodious warble not unlike a bluebird's, I remember it from high in the mountains in June, and suddenly recognize the song of the Townsend's solitaire.

After nesting in June or July, the solitaires move down from the boreal mountaintops to the desert foothills, where they spend the winter. In autumn they sing in unison, as though to say: "Here am I, where are you?" But the question remains, why do they sing? They cannot be announcing their claim to a territory at this time of year. I believe they sing as a response to the sun, from which all life flows, in sheer exuberance of spirit. To the scientist, however, the notion of sun worship is unacceptable when imputed to creatures less intelligent than he. Offering what he considers a more logical explanation for the singing of birds in the fall, he says that as part of the cycle of the solar year, the onset of migration, song, and mating in spring is in response to the increased intensity of light from the sun as the earth swings around the ecliptic, and that in autumn when the light is dwindling it passes through the same degree of intensity that initiated the cycle six months earlier. September, he says, is a false spring to which birds respond, though in a lesser degree, as they did to the true spring in March or April. But although this explanation may be scientifically acceptable, it does not account for bird song throughout the winter months, when white-crowned sparrows whistle at dawn and dusk from the willow thickets where they roost for the night. And when the solitaire sings at noon during a January thaw, whether he is or is not a sun-worshiper is a distinction of little moment. Why should he not be? We human beings are all sun-worshipers: we have no choice. The physicist who works to harness the energy of the sun with a thermonuclear device is a sun-worshiper in a very practical sense, whether or not he will admit it. When science reaches beyond the phenomena of nature into metaphysics, it enters a realm where such distinctions lose their meaning.

The solitaire is not alone in his response to the light. House finches also sing from their high perch on television aerials, their rosy throats glowing in the sun. In the brown fields, invisible among the dead stalks, Western meadowlarks gurgle melodiously. Robins too sing on winter days when the sun is warm, and when we ourselves are half deluded into believing that spring is on the way.

The birds that appear first in the fall have been driven from their cool summer homes at high altitudes by freezing weather. Some, such as the cerulean mountain bluebird, have been forced by their insectivorous habits to come in search of dormant pupae, the eggs and resting stages of insects and spiders. Juncos and white-crowned sparrows come to feast on the tiny seeds of the chamise. Clark's nutcrackers make their appearance in late September, when the opening of the pitchy piñon cones reveals the brown fruit nestled inside. Along with them come the Steller's and piñon jays, both of which like to feed on the topmost cones of the piñon pines.

During the greater part of the year, foraging bands of piñon jays roam the low foothills and juniper flats. As winter approaches, these groups gradually coalesce into flocks of several hundred. When September comes around, these flocks are already well developed. During the period which in New Mexico amounts to a second spring, when the arroyos between the ridges are golden with a variety of blossoming herbaceous plants and shrubs, the jays begin to appear near my house in undisciplined troops that eventually become a sort of ragged confederation. Alighting in the cottonwood trees, they caw noisily while they look the place over. Although they have been here before and will return when natural forage becomes scarce, they do not yet approach my feeder, whose contents are not to their liking. On a sudden unanimous impulse they all take off in a straggling flock, still conversing.

Although the behavior of piñon jays is affected by the seasons, they are nonmigratory birds, and do not even change their habitat to the same degree as the nutcrackers and Steller's jays, which migrate vertically between the high mountains and the foothills. In this respect the piñon jays are like their relatives the scrub jays (*Woodhousei*), which live all year round in the piñon–juniper region. Whether they have developed as sophisticated a means of communication as their similarly gregarious relatives the crows has not been determined. But it would appear that the isolating influence of territorial claims that affects the mated pairs of most bird species has been attenuated, permitting cooperative associations such as the presence of a third adult bird as a helper at the nest.

As I sit at my typewriter on a winter morning, I can look out through my studio window at the low hills to the northeast while a flock of piñon jays makes its circuit of the feeding grounds in the Tesuque valley; they know where all the handouts are, and often they fly directly over the studio shortly after sunrise. They sail down from the hills in groups of less than ten, until the entire flock of more than a hundred birds has gathered in the cottonwood trees near the house. Here they often sit for a while, "mewing," "quehing," and "whawking," before they settle on the feeder in a blue, squabbling mass. After they have gorged themselves, they fly back in straggling columns to the hill from which they have come.

As the weather becomes frostier with the approach of winter, bluebirds begin to appear: the all-blue mountain bluebird, which commonly nests among the firs and aspens at the same altitude as the solitaire, and the Western bluebird, which differs from the Eastern species in being marked with chestnut on its back as well as on its breast. Traveling in groups and small flocks that stay together, the bluebirds are easily recognized by their gentle, piping calls and by the peculiar, wing-flicking fight that is characteristic of thrushes, including the solitaire. The Western bluebird, like its Eastern counterpart, nests in hollow trees or old holes made by sapsuckers. In the valleys they are also particularly attracted to rundown apple orchards, where they find an abundance of nesting sites. Once I found a mountain bluebird nesting well below its usual altitude, in a hollow in an adobe wall under the eaves of a barn, and I found another building its nest in the deserted burrow of a ground squirrel in the steep side of an arroyo.

In spring when nesting begins, bluebirds and scrub jays have both acquired their brightest plumage. All three species go through a postnuptial molt in summer, leaving their plumage grayer and more somber. Mountain bluebirds, clear azure in spring, are slaty blue following this molt, leaving the sexes less easily distinguished and more like the juveniles. From intense purplish ultramarine, the Western bluebird has become quite drab; even the chestnut on the back is less conspicuous. The scrub jay is less affected by the summer molt, although its hue is noticeably less brilliant. The adults of this species do not molt in the spring; instead, the conspicuous spring plumage is acquired by the wearing down of the duller-colored feather tips that had concealed the intenser blue underneath. The transformation is gradual and unnoticed until we begin to feel spring in our bones.

During the winter, flocks of strange birds occasionally appear in the cottonwood groves along the watercourses that drain the western slopes of the Sangre de Cristo range. They come unexpectedly to stay a few hours or days, departing with as little forewarning as they came. Notable among these erratic visitors is the evening grosbeak, whose migration routes, breeding grounds, and wintering localities are continually shifting. Members of the species may be abundant one year and absent the next, or they may come and go during the same season, especially during the winter months. For nesting they seem to prefer the coniferous forest, either high in the mountains of the West or among the firs of northern Michigan, Minnesota, and Canada. But even in this they are not consistent. In New Mexico the first intimation of their abrupt arrival is often a multitudinous chirping, like that of English sparrows, from the tops of the cottonwood trees. Perched there in the dead of winter, they may sit for hours simply talking among themselves. If they arrive in spring after the sap has begun to rise, they feed on the swollen leaf buds—though without causing appreciable harm to the trees. They are usually not interested in the bird seed I put out, which attracts other birds in large numbers. However, as confirmation of their unpredictable behavior, one year a large flock stayed around for weeks, eating enormous quantities of cracked corn that I spread in the driveway. Sometimes they appear at sunrise to drink from the pool I keep unfrozen all winter with an electric heater. At such times they can be seen at best advantage, and the differences between the sexes are easily discernible. Across the forehead above the massive, greenish-white beak, the male has a band of lemon yellow extending backward as a superciliary stripe. The crown is black and the feathers of the neck, throat, and cheeks are dark olive brown fading to olive yellow on the backs, sides, and breast. The tail and primary wing feathers are jet black, but all the secondary wing feathers—as though by a capricious afterthought—are immaculately white. When the bird is perched, these large white patches and the huge, light-colored beak are its most conspicuous features. The female grosbeak is much less gaudily marked: her dark head is without the yellow band, and its color blends into a soft, silvery gray along the back, becoming lighter toward the tail—which is itself a much darker gray,

GOLDEN-WINGED WARBLER ♂ *Vermivora chrysoptera* (Jackson, Michigan: 1960)

CERULEAN WARBLER ♀♂ *Dendroica cerulea* (Jackson, Michigan: 1960)

TENNESSEE WARBLER ♂ *Vermivora peregrina* (Ely, Minnesota: 1961)

CAPE MAY WARBLER ♀♂ *Dendroica tigrina* (Ely, Minnesota: 1961)

108

OVENBIRD *Seiurus aurocapillus* (Ely, Minnesota: 1961)

WILSON'S WARBLER ♂ *Wilsonia pusilla* (Brainard Lake, Colorado: 1961)

CONNECTICUT WARBLER ♀♂ *Oporornis agilis* (Ely, Minnesota: 1962)

TOWNSEND'S SOLITAIRE *Myadestes townsendi* (Sangre de Cristo Mountains, New Mexico: 1953)

as are the wings. The aggressive appearance of evening grosbeaks does not belie their behavior. Coming to drink in the morning, they drive away all the robins and even attack one another.

A less frequent visitant, and the only other bird whose wanderings are equally erratic, is the Bohemian waxwing. Late one winter a few years ago, a large flock mysteriously appeared in our Chinese elms and cottonwoods, where its members spent several days feasting on the winter buds. The number of waxwings around Santa Fe must have been very large, since they were reported simultaneously by many observers. Unlike its smaller relative the cedar waxwing, the Bohemian waxwing is generally confined to the Western states. It breeds in the boreal forest, and roams widely over the Rocky Mountain area throughout the rest of the year. Both waxwings are sleek, fawn-colored birds with neat, unruffled, pointed crests. The Western species is the darker of the two, and differs also in possessing white wing markings and rusty undertail feathers. The presence of red, waxlike tips on the wing feather margins is not an invariable attribute of either species. On the occasion I have mentioned, it was their voices that first drew my attention to the presence of a flock of waxwings—a continuous sibilance overhead, such as a swarm of very large noisy gnats might make, which caused me to look up and find the trees covered with birds. At first I thought they were cedar waxwings; but the sound had a hoarse, grating timbre, and unlike the clear, monosyllabic *zeee* of that species, it consisted of two syllables, the first very short: *zereee.* With field glasses I noted immediately the white on the wings and the rusty feathers under the tail, and knew the visitors were Bohemian waxwings although I had never seen one before.

As the days grow warmer with the approach of spring, the house finches begin to sing in earnest, and to investigate all their favorite nesting sites: the lamp by the front door, the open Mexican birdcage that hangs on the wall under the west portal. These first signs of courtship are premature; nest-building by the house finches will not begin seriously for another month. Another sign of the imminence of spring is the trilling of plain titmice as they explore cracks and crannies and broken-down woodpecker holes with an eye to setting up a household. But it is not until the Say's phoebes appear and begin their frantic courtship, trilling sweetly in unison as they flutter seductively around the portals, that one can be sure the cold weather is over for another season. And on the day when the rattle of hummingbird wings cuts through the air, one can be confident that spring has truly arrived in New Mexico.

Five For several years after taking up residence in New Mexico, I began my photographic activities each April with a search for desert horned larks. I spent many hours observing these birds, recording their activities in detail as well as photographing them. I had never met with any birds like them, and I found their behavior near their nests endlessly fascinating. Other horned larks of North America have the curious habit of collecting small pebbles and arranging them on one side of the nest as a kind of paved doorstep. The function of this habit is as obscure as that of the red-breasted nuthatch in smearing pitch around its nesting hole. In the grassland areas of New Mexico where I have studied horned larks, the adobe soil contains very little gravel, so that they use lumps of clay instead. They approach the nest by running along the ground, a manner less likely than any other to reveal the nest's location. Sometimes they make low reconnoitering flights before settling on the ground a dozen yards away, often to stand upright for minutes on end as they peer over a clump of weeds. Reassured at last, a lark will dart forward with lowered head from one tuft of grass to the next. To keep one always in view requires unwavering attention, since their pinkish color blends with the soil as they freeze into immobility, making the camouflage almost perfect. Then, if its position has not been carefully noted, the bird is not easily found again.

Equally interesting is the behavior of piñon jays in protecting their young from predators. I have never seen a piñon jay fly directly to its nest, to the tree in which it is situated, or even to one close by; nor have I ever seen one perch in the top of the nest tree. The behavior of scrub jays is similarly secretive, although I have found their nests by watching them through glasses from a hillside, noting where they perched and then searching all the trees in the area.

For two years, scrub jays nested in the honeysuckle vines beside the kitchen door of my house in New Mexico, repairing the old nest the second year. They became so tame that the female could be stroked while she incubated her eggs, and later it was possible for one to put a hand on the nest while they fed their young. A pair of these jays also nested in a piñon pine near the house. On June 3, 1948, when the nest contained five young birds near fledging age, I set up my camera and flash equipment nearby. Since these birds were much more timid, and had not come to the nest while I was in sight, I had set up a blind from which to operate the camera. The adults were now feeding their young very infrequently—an indication that the time of fledging was imminent, and that the parents were trying to induce them to leave the nest by withholding food.

I had waited for an hour and a half, during which neither adult came to the nest, when a sharpshinned hawk alighted on the nest tree. Immediately I became alert for a dramatic event, though I did not know quite what to expect. Would the jays defend their nest, or would I be a witness to an unopposed act of predation? The latter was what happened, but not in a manner to produce a once-in-a-lifetime photographic opportunity. The jays remained quiet until the hawk flew down to a lower branch, when one of them started crying out vociferously. When the hawk moved to a perch directly behind the nest, I expected its next move would be to hop onto the side of the nest. Instead, almost before I realized what was happening, the hawk swiftly and silently reached out one taloned foot, seized a young jay by the head, and flew off with it. For a moment the parent jays ceased their clamor, and the other young jays were as silent as the predator itself; its victim had probably been killed instantly. As soon as the sharpshin had taken wing, however, the adult jays began crying out in unmistakable agitation as they flew after it for several hundred yards.

When they returned from their hopeless pursuit, the adults did not go to the nest. The four remaining young birds now became increasingly restless until one by one they hopped onto the

114

edge of the nest, into the surrounding branches, and finally to the ground. The removal of one of their number, by reducing the accustomed pressure of close quarters, had perhaps hastened their departure from the nest.

Another time in New Mexico, likewise a photographic failure, I was attempting to photograph long-tailed chats in a willow thicket on the flood banks of the Rio Grande. Like the jays, these birds were so extremely timid that I had resorted to a blind; but even then they would not accept my equipment. I had removed most of it from near the nest and had begun to set it up again, piece by piece, when the chats set up the unmistakable, querulous complaint that always indicates the presence of a snake. I could see none, however, nor could I be sure whether it was approaching along the ground or over the tops of bushes, as some snakes are quite capable of doing. Even though I was very much on the alert, I was completely taken by surprise when I saw that this one had zeroed in over the willow tree containing the chats' nest and was now poised there, looking down at the young birds. The thought came to me of what a dramatic picture I might have gotten, had my equipment been in operation, as I watched the sinuous, copper-colored length twined among the willow stems, arching over to reveal the pale yellow-pink of the belly scales, its head aimed like an arrow at the young birds below. Then I rushed from the blind and drove it off—a Rio Grande red racer at least five feet long. But I did not know how persistent snakes can be. In twenty minutes it was back; three times I chased it from the nest, and three times it slithered off over the willow branches without going all the way to the ground, and with a speed that lived up to its name. The fourth time, my determination fed by anger, I caught and killed it. Then, somewhat ashamed of my own interference with the ways of nature, I packed up my camera and equipment and left.

This was not my only experience with snakes. At the Santa Anna Refuge in southern Texas I had found the nest of a hooded oriole beautifully situated among low-hanging festoons of Spanish moss. Having waited to begin photography until the young orioles were five days old, I arrived early in the morning to find a blue racer draped among the moss, its head inside the nest. Its bulging coils were proof that the last of the young orioles was even then in the process of being swallowed. In a mixture of disgust and disappointment I shook the branch from which the moss hung, and the racer let itself down and sped away on the ground.

Another time, in Florida, I came upon two chicken snakes in the act of cleaning out a martin colony from several old woodpecker holes in a dead tree. The snakes, coiled together and hanging from the entrance to the lowest of the nests, were so engorged with their meal that they each looked like a stocking stuffed with tennis balls. The smooth and barkless surface of the tree, in which they were too high to be reached and from which they could not be disloged by pounding on it, raised the question of how the snakes had managed to climb it.

During my sojourn in south Texas I found a coot's nest in a cattail marsh at the edge of a small pond. Since the water was too deep for a blind but not deep enough for a tripod, I decided on a procedure that had worked well in a similar situation, years before, at a small Illinois prairie marsh inhabited by red-winged blackbirds. While I moved through the cattails, counting the redwings, I flushed a marsh bird from a nest containing eight sparsely speckled, buffy eggs. Since she went off quickly through the reeds, I could not identify her; but from the eggs, which were smaller than a bittern's and not immaculate, I guessed her to be a Virginia rail. Because of the reputed timidity of rails, I surmised that an attempt at photographing the owner of the nest would not succeed, and decided on another strategy. This was to place a triggering device, concealed in a split section of dried cattail stalk, in the nest in such a way that the rail would press against it and release the shutter as she settled over her eggs. The scheme would undoubtedly be a one-time affair if it worked at all, since following the trauma of the first exposure it was unlikely that the bird would return a second time so long as the camera and lamps remained in place. Nor was there any way to ensure that the bird would be in the most satisfactory position at the moment of exposure. Nevertheless, concluding that nothing risked meant nothing gained, the next day I set up my camera with the triggering device in the nest, and then walked to higher ground on the far side of the small marsh to watch what happened. I hadn't been there long when I saw the flash and knew that mechanically, at least, the device had worked. Later, the picture of a Virginia rail arranging her eggs proved that the effort was justified.

Such was the device I intended to try with the coot. Setting it up as I had before, I went away and waited several hours before returning to see whether a photograph had been taken in the meantime. No bird slipped away into the cattails as I waded out to the camera, and my first thought was that she had deserted. Then I saw that the nest was empty. Evidently a predator had come and eaten the eggs. Its identity was a mystery, since there were no broken eggs, fragments of shells, or signs of their contents to be seen: the nest was as tidy as though it had just been completed. In my bafflement, it did not immediately occur to me that I might have a record of what had happened. And indeed the processed film revealed the predator: an indigo snake in the act of swallowing one of the eggs, all of which it had eaten whole.

Hawks and snakes are not alone in their taste for the eggs and young of birds. Crows and jays both share it. The experience of having tame scrub jays at my doorstep in New Mexico has only somewhat tempered my own longstanding antipathy toward the bluejays of Great Spruce Head Island. Part of the antipathy, I confess, is a result of their having spoiled so many photographic opportunities for me by their depredations on the nests of smaller birds. With good cause, bluejays appear to be heartily disliked by their potential victims. Wherever a jay goes, it is likely to be followed by the protesting complaints of lesser forest species, which may go as far as to launch a swooping attack—as I have seen a pugnacious olive-sided flycatcher do. Through it all, the jays' attitude remains one of studied disdain or indifference.

I put the blame on bluejays for tearing away the loose bark behind which a pair of brown creepers had built their nest in the spring of 1969. The creepers had chosen a dead balsam standing in the open, its bark hanging in ragged sheets about a lean, bleaching trunk. The jays must have been on the watch while the nest was being built in order to have found that nest. What appears to have been the same fate overtook a family of tree swallows that had made the unfortunate decision to nest in a long-abandoned flicker hole in a dead white birch. Since the wood had rotted away behind the still intact bark, the jays had little difficulty in penetrating it and devouring the young swallows. Another pair of swallows I watched in the process of choosing a nest site had better luck. They had chosen a year-old downy woodpecker hole in a dead spruce, which was still solid. While they were probing and considering its merits, a downy woodpecker happened to alight on the tree. Since for the swallows the tree was now their territory, one of them showed its intense displeasure by diving at the woodpecker in short, swift lunges. The woodpecker, evidently feeling that he had an equal claim to the tree, ducked around it at each lunge, thus frustrating the attacker. The swallow's mate now joined the combat, and their concerted tactic of diving at the newcomer from two sides succeeded in driving him away.

Evidence of predation by bluejays is not lacking. One episode in which I observed it at first hand occurred while I was in the midst of photographing a pair of nesting redstarts. While the pair went off to gather food for their young, there was little for me to do except observe what went on around me from my position in an alder thicket. It was during one of these periods that I heard the mewing notes of a pair of red-eyed vireos that indicate extreme distress—a sound such as many species of birds utter when the situation is desperate, as the chats I have described had done when their nest was threatened by a snake. I have heard flickers driven to the ground and cornered by an accipiter give the same cry of terror. Attracted by the sound, I have several times driven off the hawk, whereupon the flicker's equanimity returned at once.

At the cries of the vireos, other birds soon joined in: a catbird mewed, whitethroats scolded, several warblers uttered excited chipping notes, goldfinches whined and squeaked, and a pair of Acadian chickadees added their *wheeze dee dee dee* to the chorus. In the distance, a thrush began its *puck puck.* Compelled by the same morbid attraction that brings human spectators to the scene of an accident, birds gathered from all directions, and as the commotion grew louder, led by the vireos, the crowd came flying in my direction. It was then that I saw the silhouette of a large bird moving deliberately from tree to tree above the vireos. My first thought was that it must be a crow; but when the predator alighted in the top branches of a birch tree almost directly overhead, I recognized it as a bluejay. Held in its beak was a young bird, still wriggling and twitching. Having eluded the protesting parents, the jay now proceeded to transfer its prey to the grasp of one foot against the branch, where it hammered at it with its bill. When the wriggling ceased, the jay flew off again with its now dead victim.

Bluejays, starlings, bronzed grackles and cowbirds are all relative newcomers to the avifauna of Great Spruce Head Island. Since the species was misguidedly introduced into the United States in 1890, the aggressive starling has spread throughout the continent in ever growing numbers. I suspect, though without incontrovertible evidence, that starlings account for much of the nest-robbing against warblers, flycatchers, and tree swallows on the island. Certainly they are aggressive enough when it comes to pre-empting nesting sites from tree swallows and flickers, or appropriating them from already established residents. Flickers have the worst of it, since the cavities they chisel out are almost exactly the right size for a nesting starling. Three years ago I found five china-white eggs, two of them cracked and the other three apparently undamaged, lying on the ground below a flicker hole in a spruce stub which I had been observing. Presumably the eggs had been removed by starlings in search of a nesting site. How they had managed to do so without more damage is a mystery, although what I have seen gulls do with eider eggs— about which I shall have something to say presently—suggests the answer. That particular effort by the starlings was unsuccessful, since the flickers returned, laid more eggs, and reared a family.

The increase of bronzed grackles, a species generally more at home around farmland and developed areas than climax forest, is harder to account for than that of the starling. So far as its predatory habits are concerned, however, analyses of stomach contents and eyewitness accounts in ornithological literature have indicated its role in pillaging the nests of smaller birds.

The cowbird's habits are, of course, not predatory but parasitic. The influx of this species on the island was apparent to me in the large number of parasitized nests I began to discover after years of seeing no such evidence in the nest of potential hosts. The increase is so great that the chance of finding a young cowbird or a foreign egg in the nest of a warbler or an alder flycatcher on the island is approaching 50 percent.

Over the period of nearly sixty years since I first become acquainted with Great Spruce Head Island, many changes have taken place. Forests have grown up where meadows once sloped down to white gravel beaches. Mature stands of coniferous forest have been flattened by winter gales, opening the ground to the light and making way for a new generation of seedlings that race upward, growing more than a foot in a single season. The changes in the forest cover have been accompanied by a corresponding gradual shift in the bird fauna. In the early 1920s, hermit and Swainson's thrushes were extremely common. To the liquid cadence of their voices at twilight would be added the crystalline, repeated syllables of the white-throated sparrow. Adding the final poignant effect, a woodcock rising from the edge of a wet pasture and then fluttering back to earth would give voice to its faint, warbled song, whose mystery is greater than any other.

In recent years the thrush population, except for robins, has declined greatly. Within the last decade, Swainsons have become scarce and the hermit thrush is no longer a summer resident. The veery, which for a while during the 1960s seemed to be replacing the hermit thrush, has now also disappeared. With the replacement of yellow and white birches and other hardwood trees by coniferous forests, red-eyed vireos have gone the way of the thrushes. Meanwhile, those of their congeners that are more at home among evergreens appear to be moving in. Since 1968 I have seen solitary vireos—a new species for the island—during three seasons, and have twice found their nests. Among warblers now present as summer residents, although not in the past, are the blackburnian, bay-breasted, and Canada. They are replacing others such as the magnolia and Nashville, and to a limited degree the black-throated green warbler. The greatest change, however—even greater than the influx of cowbirds, starlings, and bronzed grackles—has been in the arrival during the last ten years of purple finches and red crossbills in prodigious numbers, accompanied by smaller numbers of white-winged crossbills and occasionally by pine grosbeaks.

Although changes in vegetation have had their effect on the bird life of Great Spruce Head Island, the factor of changes as a result of human agency can also be observed. And although disaster such as has overtaken the bird life of other areas has not occurred on the Maine coast, signs of its imminence already loom on the horizon. The once abundant osprey population has shrunk in Penobscot Bay from hundreds to a mere handful: in 1913 seventeen pairs nested on the island, whereas there were two in 1971, and in 1969 there had been none at all. Prosperous gull and tern colonies that once covered innumerable small islands and mainland ledges have all but disappeared. The rookeries of great blue and black-crowned night herons that filled me with awe when I visited them half a century ago have ceased to exist.

So far as I know, the only seabirds to have increased significantly during that half century are the eider ducks. During my youth they were present in small numbers on the remote, barren outer islands; since then they have increased prodigiously, moving up the bay in spring to nest along the shores of all the islands. By the last week in May, the time I usually arrive in Penobscot Bay, most of the eiders have paired and many of the females are already sitting, on clutches numbering from three to five enormous, greenish eggs, in nests lined with gray down. Others are still being courted by the gaudy black-and-white drakes, whom they coyly ignore. At low tide, much of their time is spent swimming about the seaweed–covered rocks; at high tide, they roost on the dry ledges. As pair formation is completed, fewer and fewer females are observed out on the water—only those whose first attempts at nesting have been interrupted by the predation of black-backed and herring gulls, pausing before a second attempt. By now the drakes have gathered into flocks as they prepare to depart for the outer islands, where they are resident the year round except for this short breeding interlude inshore.

The incubation period lasts twenty-five days—which means that allowing for late starters and second or third attempts at nesting, the breeding season covers almost two months. The numbers of eider ducks have increased even though their enemies take a heavy toll of eggs and young each year, probably because the life span of an eider that has reached adulthood may extend over many seasons. Crows and ravens prey on eiders, taking mainly their eggs; but throughout the breeding season the most persistent predators are gulls. When gull colonies still thrived in the bay, I spent much time in late spring photographing them from a blind set in the midst of a colony. Thus I had ample opportunity to observe what went on between the gulls and those eiders so unforesighted as to attempt to raise their ducklings here.

The great black-backed gulls, being considerably larger than the herring gulls—on whom they also preyed with what seemed to me a cannibalistic disregard for kinship—destroyed most of the eiders' eggs. Generally one of these gulls would hammer away at the unguarded eggs in a nest until the shell cracked, drinking up whatever fraction of its liquid contents wasn't immediately spilled out and lost.

During these solitary photographic expeditions, I began to learn the effects of human trespassers on such island colonies. By landing and setting up a blind, I had frightened several ducks off their nests along with scores of gulls. But the gulls, whose boldness was reinforced by their numbers as compared with the solitary timidity of the ducks, soon returned. The advantage of flight over swimming, a more cautious approach favored by the eiders, also served the gulls. As a result, the eiders' nests were unprotected for long periods after the gulls had settled down on their nests or were strutting about bugling in their usual fashion. Thus it was inevitable that not a few eider nests, including even some of those on which the female was actually sitting, would be discovered by gulls on the prowl.

From my blind I watched an eider nest being raided simultaneously by a great black-backed and a herring gull. Despite the size of the eider's eggs, which are considerably larger than their own, a gull of either species is able to hold an egg crosswise in its bill and walk or fly off with it. What looks like an uncomfortable stretch is required, but in this manner the egg can be held just behind the slight hook of the upper mandible.

I have also watched from a blind while crows destroyed unguarded eider nests. Indeed, in early spring crows gather on these treeless islands, which otherwise offer them little, simply to prey on the ducks. Sloop Island, where I set up a blind in 1939 to photograph the great black-backed gulls—and where I made most of these observations—is a chain of three grass-covered rocky islets or tombolos connected by gravel bars. I began my observations while the eiders and blackbacks were both incubating, and before many of the herring gulls had laid eggs. Between May 29 and June 2, during three days spent on the island, I saw two-thirds of the duck nests I had counted on the first day destroyed. A pair of crows had built a nest, possibly to take advantage of a readily available food supply, in a crevice of rock just above the high tide line. They laid four eggs, but the nest was washed away in a storm; so much for the foresight of that undertaking.

In bird colonies where dominant and minority species associate, some very strange things can happen. Occasionally, for example, eiders will be found making use of gulls' grass nests from the previous year as a foundation for their own. If their eggs are laid before lining the nest with down, a gull may usurp the site before the start of incubation and lay her eggs alongside the duck's. I have found gulls' nests containing both gull and eider eggs, and suspect that the gull could incubate them both. If the ducks have feathered their adopted nests, however, it is likely that the gulls will destroy the eggs and remove the lining. In view of the ability of gulls to carry off a duck's egg, it is also possible than eider eggs found in a gull's nest may have been placed there by the gull.

Besides eating the eggs, gulls also prey on young ducklings. The most vulnerable period for the latter is at the time of hatching, before they have dried off and been led down to the water. Any disturbance of the female at this time may mean the loss of her whole brood. Even after they have reached the water, the ducklings are secure only if they stay close to their mother. A stray in the midst of a gull colony is not long for this world, as a drama I once witnessed made all too clear. It involved a duckling that had become separated from its siblings soon after it entered the water. In a valiant but one-sided struggle for survival, it was doing its best to catch up with its mother when a black-backed gull spotted and swooped down on it. Seeing the threat, the duckling dived beneath the surface, whereupon the gull swerved off and circled for another look while the duckling bobbed up. Another swoop and another quick dive followed, but the downy little bird was too buoyant to stay under water for long and popped up too soon. On the third dive, the gull plunged after it head first, to appear seconds later holding in its bill a limp and bedraggled duckling, with which it flew toward shore to a chorus of excited trumpeting by other gulls.

As the hatchlings increase in numbers, the females and their broods join forces and in so doing find security in numbers. They form rafts containing as many as several dozen adults and anywhere from a third to half as many ducklings, which are escorted along the rocky shore at low tide to feed on the small crustaceans and annelids they find under the lank brown seaweed and the barnacle-encrusted rocks. That the adult females so far outnumber the young in these nursery congregations is a measure of the loss by predation. The entire broods of some birds have been wiped out; others may have lost all but one or two. While the ducklings conducted by their mothers nibble at the barnacles, the old birds without offspring cruise along the shore, keeping a constant alert against danger. With the appearance of a human figure near at hand, the guard ducks set up a great quacking and rapidly swim farther out. The mothers gather their chicks about them and also swim away from shore—but no faster than the young ones are capable of following. Very young ducklings huddle close to their mother's tail for safety the way children hold their parents' hands in a crowd, and paddle along vigorously, bobbing in her wake. If the danger appears still greater, those females without ducklings abandon their responsibility to take off with a noisy clatter and splashing of wings, leaving behind a trail of foam while the deserted mothers fend alone for their young and themselves. The maternal instinct is so strong that those with young remain without regard for the risk to themselves, encouraging the ducklings and leading them out into deep water. Once in a while a duckling will become separated from the other members of the brood; then, on a clucking signal from its mother, it will scoot after her, using both feet and wings in a burst of energy that seems literally to lift it off the surface of the water. The kinship of ducklings to parents is sorted out in these times of emergency, as they leave the common group to join the adult to whom, by the process known among students of animal behavior as imprinting, they were conditioned to attach themselves at the time of hatching.

Social life within an assemblage of female eiders finds expression in continuous vocalization, which in anthropomorphic terms suggests the gossipy chatter of a cocktail party. Low-pitched quackings and mutterings are interrupted every so often by a *whoo whoo* or, less frequently, by a hoarse, guttural *arrroo*. These utterances are not aggressive, but appear to serve a communicative function, helping to cement the social ties within the flock. From time to time a duck, an immature yearling or a solitary drake that has remained behind with the female flock, will rise out of the water on its tail and vigorously flap its wings. The function of this behavior, which is usually performed by two or more birds in succession, is apparently to relieve latent aggression, or possibly it announces residual territorial claims as a substitute for actual physical confrontation.

On a windless day, when a gray blanket of fog over the bay obscures all but the nearest landmarks, softening all details of rocks and trees on the shore to faint silhouettes, the moist atmosphere carries the calling of gulls and the muted grumbling of ducks for long distances over the surface of the water. Arriving out of the fog, these sounds of nature, like those of auto horns or the throb of motors, reach the ears of the listener as though from no direction. But the

KENTUCKY WARBLER ♀♂ *Oporornis formosus* (Miami–Whitewater Wildlife Preserve, Ohio: 1963)

YELLOW-BREASTED CHAT *Icteria vireus* (Miami–Whitewater Wildlife Preserve, Ohio: 1963)

BELTED KINGFISHER ♂ *Megaceryle alcyon* (Pittsburg, New Hampshire: 1965)

WORM-EATING WARBLER ♀ ♂ *Helmithéros vermivorus* (Kanawha State Park, West Virginia: 1971)

SHORT-BILLED MARSH WREN *Cistothorus platensis* (Winnetka, Illinois: 1942)

126   HENSLOW'S SPARROW *Passerherbulus henslowii* (Jackson, Michigan: 1961)

EASTERN MEADOWLARK *Sturnella magna* (Winnetka, Illinois: 1941)

ROCK WREN *Salpinctes obsoletus* (Tesuque, New Mexico: 1962)

HORNED LARK *Eremophila alpestris* (Santa Fe, New Mexico: 1951)

GREEN-TAILED TOWHEE *Chlorura chlorura* (Santa Fe Basin, New Mexico: 1952)

LAZULI BUNTING ♀♂ *Passerina amoena* (Tesuque, New Mexico: 1960)

PAINTED BUNTING ♂ *Passerina ciris* (Homestead, Florida: 1954)

OREGON JUNCO *Junco oreganus* (Tesuque, New Mexico: 1947)

INDIGO SNAKE EATING EGGS OF AMERICAN COOT (near San Benito, Texas: 1947)

VIRGINIA RAIL *Rallus limicola* (Wheeling, Illinois: 1947-48)

SCRUB JAY *Aphelocoma coerulescens* (Tesuque, New Mexico: 1961)

curtailment of vision enhances what can be heard on such days; the hush produced by the fog among the forest birds, and its damping effect on all background noises, seems to foster the transmission of the slightest sound. The effect for the ducks may not be the same, however, since they appear to be less alert to danger from the land on foggy days. At such times, where the shore is screened by trees, I have been able to take advantage of this barrier, creeping down behind it to where I could view ducklings feeding with their mothers at closer range than would be possible in clear weather. Under such conditions the peeping of the baby ducks, the faint scraping of their bills as they nibble at the barnacles, and the gentle murmuring of the mothers are audible. The close view also permits observation of their method of feeding. It is not all done at the surface. Since at halftide most of the barnacle rocks are submerged, in order to feed on the associated marine life the ducks may dive, as they do with seemingly little difficulty in spite of their buoyancy. Looking down on them from above, I have been able to observe this achievement. They submerge head first and paddle with their feet to barnacles not hidden by rockweed a foot or two below the surface. To stay in position under water, the little ducks are forced to paddle continuously. After grazing for less than a minute, they pop up like corks. As they break the surface, their downy backs are covered with silvery beads, which quickly roll off like droplets of mercury.

The juvenile down is a nearly perfect insulation because of an oily property that makes it unwettable and thus able to hold air. Not all aquatic birds are characterized by plumage impervious to water. Some, notably the anhingas or snakebirds and the cormorants, which do their fishing under water and are not less at home there than ducks, must return to land periodically to dry off. Along the coast of Maine, the silhouette of a black cormorant perched atop a spar buoy with wings spread and held motionless in heraldic fashion is a common sight.

The first explorers of our continent's northeastern shores reported in amazement a sight that is now gone forever: the teeming hordes of the great auk, a flightless, penguinlike bird that occupied every rocky niche and ledge along the coasts of Greenland and Labrador. But the entire species had been bludgeoned into extinction by ships' crews who packed the battered bodies into hogsheads to be rendered into cooking oil. The same fate overtook the less numerous Labrador duck and the superabundant passenger pigeon, whose migrating flocks once darkened the Midwestern skies like storm clouds, and which were exterminated for use as pig food and fertilizer and as a mere target for the sport of killing.

Early in this century, American and snowy egrets were brought near to extinction by the depredations of plume hunters. They were saver from this fate in the nick of time by the action of the United States Congress, as a response to an aroused public feeling, in declaring the importation and interstate traffic in plumes illegal. Under the protection of this and other laws guarding against the disturbance of these and other birds, the egrets have regained much of their former abundance in the Everglades region of southern Florida. But many other species of birds are barely surviving, or are slowly losing their fight for survival because of curtailment of a favorable territory in which to carry on their breeding functions, to rest during migratory flights, or to find food during the winter. The California condor, the whooping crane, and several varieties of prairie chickens have been losing ground not so much because of persecution by man as through the gradual attrition of their ancestral habitats. Until recently, however, most birds have not been directly threatened by the activities of man. Even though enormous tracts of land have been cleared in the Midwestern states, the total number of birds does not appear to have diminished. Certain forest species, including some varieties of woodpeckers, nuthatches, hawks, and owls, are undoubtedly rarer. On the other hand, birds that prefer semi-open country, bushy sproutland, and second-growth forest appear to have multiplied greatly. Among these are several kinds of warblers, many of the sparrows and their allies, the cuckoos, some of the thrushes, and the crows, all of which are much more plentiful than they were in pioneer days. The blue-winged, golden-winged, and chestnut-sided warblers, for example, favor sproutland and young second-growth forest as nesting habitats; song sparrows are bush- and ground-nesting birds; and robins and bluebirds are members of the thrush family which, as everyone who has lived in a suburb or on a farm knows, adapt readily to a human environment. Who is not familiar with the sight of a fat robin running in short spurts across a lawn, pausing as it cocks its head to one side—to listen, we were told as children, but much more probably to look—and all of a sudden probing deep into the soft soil to pull out, with legs braced and neck arched, a long rubbery worm?

The introduction since the end of World War II of chlorinated hydrocarbon insecticides has caused a decline in the populations of several species of birds. Some of the chemicals in this class are also toxic to plants and are used as weed-killers and defoliants. The most familiar of the insecticides is DDT. First used to control mosquitoes, it was soon discovered to be active against many orders of insects, and then belatedly to be a danger to crustaceans, fish, and birds as well. DDT and its many close chemical relatives kill by interrupting the transmission of nerve impulses, and therefore can affect a broad spectrum of organisms. Because they are substances foreign to the environment, without counterparts in nature, they are refractory to decomposition by the natural chemistry of living organisms and cannot be excreted by the organs of elimination. As a result, the animal organism as a last resort stores them in the fatty tissue, the attics and cellars of its internal structure, where they may remain for years, out of contact with vital processes, until the fats are mobilized to meet emergency demands. When this occurs, and the foreign deposits enter the circulatory system, the animal is in trouble. This is true whether the fatty tissue in which they have been stored is in the liver, kidney, bone marrow, or—most disastrous of all—the lipid elements of the nerve tissue, where they can affect the mechanisms for conducting nerve impulses so as to cause paralysis. Moreover, some of these poisons which are not completely resistant to catabolic attack may be broken down into even more toxic and resistant products, which can cause injury in concentrations a thousand times lower than the original substance.

But the worst effect of these hydrocarbons is in the way they are passed along the food chain, with often devastating effects on predatory higher animals. It is true that when an area is sprayed for mosquitoes or some other insect pest, it is unlikely that a human being, a dog, or even a bird will come in contact with enough of the poison to be injured immediately. Such may have been the reasoning first put forward as a reassurance about the harmlessness of these chemicals. The storage of hydrocarbons in their fatty tissues by carnivorous fishes may represent an increase of a millionfold over the original concentration of these chemicals in the water, from which the lower forms of life at the bottom of the food chain absorb them as fast as they appear. In turn, fish-eating birds such as grebes, loons, ospreys, and eagles may ingest massive doses of these poisons. The reproductive physiology of birds is particularly susceptible to DDT and similar chemicals, which lower fertility and eventually prevent eggshells from forming correctly.

Quite aside from these hazards, the use of organic insecticides as a way of permanently controlling insects is a futile undertaking in the end. Adaptation to changes in the environment comes about through mutations; and the rate at which mutations occur depends in turn on the rate of reproduction by the species concerned. In man, the periodicity of reproduction is about twenty years, so that centuries or even millenniums must pass before adaptation through natural selection —leaving out of consideration the possibility of future genetic engineering—becomes appreciable. For the common songbirds and other passerine species, reproductive periodicity is about one year, so that even with them evolution is too slow a process to permit the adaptation of a species to a potentially lethal change in the environment in time to save it from extinction. With insects, however, the situation is quite different. The reproductive cycle of the housefly is so short that if all the descendants of one pair lived and reproduced normally during one season from April to August, the total number would be 10^{20}, or one hundred billion billion. For the cabbage aphid, assuming an average of forty-one young per female in sixteen generations between March and October, the figure would be 10^{24} (ten thousand times one hundred billion billion). Strains of insects resistant to many of the common insecticides have been observed. At Tampa Bay, Florida, where aerial spraying was conducted for several years to control mosquitoes, it was found that increasingly high concentrations of DDT were needed to produce the same results as in the previous year. Eventually the program was discontinued; and in the meantime the destruction of fish and crustaceans in the shallow waters of the bay that the populations of herons and egrets depended on as a source of food caused them to be driven from the region—for which, incidentally, they had been a tourist attraction.

The greatest benefit that could come from the U.S. space program is not man's setting foot on the moon or Mars; it is rather the perspective he may gain on his small, vulnerable, lonely home planet. The appearance of our mottled blue-and-white sphere from thousands of miles out should make us conscious of the exceptional conditions under which the phenomenon we call life—the only life of which we have any knowledge—originated. We should be impressed by the beauty and fragility of the dynamic balance that has been preserved for so many hundreds of millions of years during which life has persisted on earth. And we should especially appreciate the shortness of our tenure on earth and use the powers we have so recently assumed to perpetuate, not destroy, the balance.

The direction that seems to promise the greatest rewards, the surest fulfillment of the hopes and aspirations of man's troubled and inquiring spirit, and of a distant and ultimate happiness, is a course of least arrogance towards his living companions—a course even less negative than the absence of superiority—a course of humble respect for life, a sympathy which sustains a recognition of the essential interdependence of all living things.

Common Crow's Nest   (Sloop Island, Maine)

Selected Bibliography

Aldrich, John W. "Habits and Habitat Differences in Two Races of Traill's Flycatcher." *The Wilson Bulletin* 65 (1953): 8-11.

Balda, Russel P., and Bateman, Gary C. "Flocking and Annual Cycle of the Pinon Jay, *Gymnorhinus Cyancephalus.*" *The Condor* 73 (1971): 287-302.

Berger, Andrew J., and Parmelee, David F. "The Alder Flycatcher in Washtenaw County, Michigan: Breeding Distribution and Cowbird Parasitism." *The Wilson Bulletin* 64 (1957): 33-38.

Hubbard, John P. "The Relationships and Evolution of the *Dendroita Coronata* Complex." *The Auk* 86 (1969): 393-432.

Kellogg, Peter Paul, and Stein, Robert Carrington. "Audio-Spectrographic Analysis of the Songs of the Alder Flycatcher." *The Wilson Bulletin* 65 (1953): 75-80.

Kendeigh, S. C. "Bird Population Studies in the Coniferous Forest Biome During a Spruce Budworm Outbreak." *Ontario Dept. Lands and Forests, Biol.,* Bull. 1, 1947.

McCabe, Robert A. "The Song and Song-flight of the Alder Flycatcher." *The Wilson Bulletin* 63 (1951): 89-98.

Mayr, Ernst. "Systematics and the Origin of the Species." *Columbia Biological Series* No. XIII, 1942.

Mengel, R. M. "The Probable History of Species Formation in Some Northern Wood Warblers (Parulidae)." *Living Bird* 3 (1964): 9-43.

Morse, Douglass H. "Competitive Relationships Between Parula Warblers and Other Species During the Breeding Season." *The Auk* 84 (1967): 490-502.

————. "The Context of Songs in Black-throated Green and Blackburnian Warblers." *The Wilson Bulletin* 79 (1967): 64-74.

————. "The Context of Songs in The Yellow Warbler." *The Wilson Bulletin* 78 (1966): 444-455.

Murie, Olaus J. "Why Do Birds Sing?" *The Wilson Bulletin* 74 (1962): 177-182.

Parkes, Kenneth C. "Traill's Flycatcher in New York." *The Wilson Bulletin* 66 (1954): 89-92.

Rand, A. L. "Glaciation, An Isolating Factor in Speciation." *Evolution* 2 (1948): 314-321.

Walkinshaw, Lawrence H. "Summer Biology of Traill's Flycatcher." *The Wilson Bulletin* 78 (1966): 31-46.

————, and Dyer, William A. "The Connecticut Warbler in Michigan." *The Auk* 78 (1961): 379-388.

Index

Virginia rail, 115-116
Virginia's warbler, 85, 86, 98, 100

Warblers, 21, 57, 84-85, 86, 117,
118, 138; Audubon's, 85, 101; bay-
breasted, 83, 118; blackburnian,
57, 59, 118; blackpoll, 57, 84;
black-throated blue, 57, 63; black-
throated gray, 84, 85, 98;
black-throated green, 57, 59, 84,
85, 118; blue-winged, 57, 61,
62, 138; Canada, 83, 84, 87,
118; Cape May, 24, 81, 82-83;
cerulean, 23, 61-63; chestnut-sided,
57, 83, 138; Connecticut, 63, 83;
golden-cheeked, 84, 85; golden-
winged, 61, 62, 138; Grace's,
60, 85, 100; hermit, 84, 85;
hooded, 22-23; hybrid, 61, 85;
Kirtland's, 60; MacGillivray's, 85,
98, 100; magnolia, 59-60, 82,
84, 86, 118; mourning, 63, 84, 85;
myrtle, 57, 59, 82, 85; Nashville,
60, 63, 82, 84; olive, 60; orange-
crowned, 85-86, 98, 100; parula,
57, 59; pileolated, 84; prairie,
60; Tennessee, 81, 83; Townsend's,
84, 85; Virginia's, 85, 86, 98,
100; Western palm, 60; Wilson's,
84; worm-eating, 84; yellow,
57, 62, 84. *See also* Chats; Ovenbird; Redstart; Water thrushes
Washington State, 85
Water thrushes, 84
Waxwings: Bohemian, 113; cedar,
82
West Virginia, 22, 84
Western bluebird, 104
Western flycatcher, 97-98, 100
Western gnatcatcher, 99-100
Western meadowlark, 98, 103
Western palm warbler, 60
Western tanager, 23-24, 98, 100
White-crowned sparrow, Gambel's,
101, 103
White-eyed vireo, 84

White-rumped shrike, 99
White-throated sparrow, 82, 101,
117, 118
Whooping crane, 137
Williamson's sapsucker, 98, 100
Wilson's warbler, 84
Winter wren, 44-45, 82
Woodcock, 118
Woodpeckers, 137; black-backed, 84;
downy, 116
Wood thrush, 84
Wood warblers, *see* Warblers
Worm-eating warbler, 84
Wrens: house, 98, 101; short-billed
marsh, 62; winter, 44-45, 82
Wright's flycatcher, 98, 99, 100

Yellow-bellied flycatcher, 83-84, 88,
97, 98
Yellow-breasted chat, 84
Yellow warbler, 57, 62, 83
Yukon territory, Canada, 85

144